Marginalism

The Economy | Key Ideas

These short primers introduce students to the core concepts, theories and models, both new and established, heterodox and mainstream, contested and accepted, used by economists and political economists to understand and explain the workings of the economy.

Published

Behavioural Economics
Graham Mallard

Degrowth
Giorgos Kallis

The Living Wage
Donald Hirsch and Laura Valadez-Martinez

Marginalism
Bert Mosselmans

The Resource Curse
S. Mansoob Murshed

Marginalism

Bert Mosselmans

agenda
publishing

First published in 2018 by Agenda Publishing

Agenda Publishing Limited
The Core
Bath Lane
Newcastle Helix
Newcastle upon Tyne
NE4 5TF
www.agendapub.com

ISBN 978-1-911116-66-0 (hardcover)
ISBN 978-1-911116-67-7 (paperback)

British Library Cataloguing-in-Publication Data
A catalogue record for this book is available from the British Library

Typeset by T&T Productions Ltd
www.tandtproductions.com

Printed and bound in the UK by TJ International

Contents

Acknowledgements

My greatest inspiration for the writing of this book came from the students of my History of Economic Thought course, which I taught in Bristol, Utrecht and Brussels, and of my courses in microeconomics, macroeconomics and industrial organization at University College Roosevelt (UCR), in which I always include elements taken from the history of economic thought. Some sections of the book were tested in my Microeconomics and Behaviour class at UCR during the fall semester of 2017. I would like to thank the participating students: Ruben van den Akker, Elikem Azumah, Evi Boel, Jurjen Bos, Vera Bruntink, Joris van Doorn, Sara Gerstner, Michel Klaassen, Emmanuel Van Lembergen, Ima Sammani and Sanne van Veen. Most of the credit, though, should go to my student assistant, Marije Sluiskes. She read the manuscript carefully and provided me with many useful comments, which helped me to greatly improve the quality of my argumentation. I would also like to thank Tobias Begeer, another UCR student, who read through the manuscript and provided valuable comments, and Sara Gerstner for redrawing the curves and tables.

I also thank the external reviewers of the manuscript for their valuable comments. My greatest thanks go to Alison Howson from Agenda Publishing and Sam Clark from T&T Productions, who edited the entire manuscript carefully and improved the quality of my writing considerably. All remaining mistakes and imperfections are obviously mine.

I hope that I have succeeded in my attempt to provide a brief introduction to the history of marginalism that can be read by a broad audience of (young) intellectuals.

1

Value, cost and price: a historical introduction to marginalism

Marginalism is a branch of economic theory that investigates what goes on at the margin of economic activity. Economic activity can be divided into producing and selling (the supply side), and consuming and enjoying (the demand side).

Let us imagine a farm that grows potatoes that are sold to and bought by the inhabitants of a small village. The amount of available fertile land is limited, which implies that the farm can only produce a certain amount of potatoes. Let us further assume that the population of the village grows, and consequently more potatoes are needed to feed the villagers. As the farm can only produce a limited number of potatoes, the inhabitants of the village will bid against each other to buy them and the farmer will be able to raise the price of the potatoes. Given that the price of potatoes has increased, the farmer may find it profitable to increase production. She may try to find additional land for cultivation, but this would require serious investment. The farmer may also try to produce more potatoes on the land she already has, by employing more labourers and/or by utilizing more equipment and manure. In either case, producing more potatoes will drive up the cost of growing each potato for the farmer. The farmer will increase her production if the additional income that she generates by selling more potatoes exceeds the additional expense required to produce them.

Economists would consider this to be the "margin" of the economic activity: the conditions under which the last potato is produced.[1] An additional potato will generate additional income or *marginal revenue*, but it will also

---

1. As we will discuss later on (chapter 7), the "marginal" unit is not necessarily the "last" unit in a temporal sense. When starting from a static point of view of the economic system, the "marginal" unit can be any unit to be removed from the system.

have to be produced using additional expenses or *marginal costs*. Therefore, when more potatoes are produced, which means that the margin is extended, the marginal cost of a potato will increase. The farmer will produce more potatoes as long as the marginal revenue from a potato exceeds the marginal cost of that potato. The marginal revenue is determined by the price that the inhabitants are willing to pay for a potato. Since potatoes are required for the survival of the inhabitants, they are in high demand. If every individual needs at least one potato per day for survival, then the inhabitants would be willing to pay a very high price to get their first essential potato. They will still be willing to pay a high price for a second potato (though a lower price than for the first), as eating just enough for survival is insufficient to preserve your health. A third potato would still be beneficial, though less essential than the second and the first, so the willingness to pay for this third potato will be lower still. Any potatoes beyond those first three could then be considered luxury items, and only relatively wealthy inhabitants would be willing to pay for them. Therefore, even though more potatoes are available, the willingness to pay for an additional potato by the inhabitants will decrease, and so will marginal revenue for the farmer. The market price of a potato will be determined by the conditions at the margin: the marginal cost of producing an additional potato, and the inhabitants' willingness to pay for this additional potato, which determines the marginal revenue for the farmer. In equilibrium, as economists like to say, marginal cost will be equal to marginal revenue: the market price for a potato is determined, on the one hand, by the marginal cost to produce the last potato, and, on the other hand, by the marginal revenue generated by this last potato, which in turn is determined by the inhabitants' willingness to pay for it. This willingness to pay is determined by the satisfaction that the consumers expect to derive from consuming the potato, and this satisfaction is called *utility* by economists.

The above is, in a nutshell, the essence of marginalism, which is at the core of contemporary microeconomic theory. Microeconomics studies, among many other things, the behaviour of both firms and consumers in order to determine the market price of goods (and services). According to marginalist economic theory, the market price of a good (or service) is determined by the conditions prevailing at the margin, as we illustrated in our potato example. On the supply side, the margin consists of the last unit that is produced, in the worst possible circumstances. On the demand side, the margin consists of the last unit that is consumed, which delivers less satisfaction or "utility" than units that were consumed before. In order to detect economic "laws" in their purest form, we must turn our attention to this margin and find out what is happening there.

This insight developed gradually throughout the nineteenth century. Adam Smith (1723–90), who is often described as the father of economics, published his *Wealth of Nations* in 1776. His work formed the basis on which authors such as David Ricardo (1772–1823), Thomas Robert Malthus (1766–1834) and John Stuart Mill (1806–73) would construct their economic theories. The time period 1776–1871 is commonly called the era of classical political economy.

In contrast to earlier writers of antiquity and the Middle Ages, these classical political economists no longer approach economic problems mainly from an ethical point of view. As we will elaborate further below, the "classics" tried to define concepts such as "value", "cost" and "price" from a theoretical point of view. Very broadly speaking, classical economists argued that the value of a good is determined by its cost of production, and they therefore devoted lots of attention to the supply side of the economy. As we will see in the next chapter, the limited availability of fertile land was a major problem for classical political economy. In that context, the theory of rent – which explains how landowners derive income from the possession of fertile land – was developed. The best-known version of the theory of rent was set up by David Ricardo. In his view, the value of a product, e.g. a potato, is determined by its cost of production at the margin, or in the worst possible circumstances (the least fertile conditions). We therefore find marginalist reasoning about the supply side in classical political economy, but the demand side did not receive much attention.

There are, however, a few (German) academic outsiders, spearheaded by Hermann Heinrich Gossen (1810–58), who are remarkable exceptions to this. Gossen realized that consumer satisfaction plays an important role in the determination of the value of a good, and therefore of its market price. The satisfaction derived from consuming an additional potato will decrease continuously when more and more potatoes are being consumed. We will explore the development of marginalism on the demand side further in chapter 3.

The year 1871 is usually seen as an important one in the history of economic thought as it saw the publication of two influential books: *The Theory of Political Economy* by William Stanley Jevons (1835–82) and *Grundsätze der Volkswirtschaftslehre* (Principles of Economics) by Carl Menger (1840–1921). In 1874 Léon Walras (1834–1940) published his *Eléments d'économie politique pure* (Elements of Pure Economics), though it was written around the same time as the books by Jevons and Menger. These three works were published independently of each other but they share a unified marginalist view of economics, taking both the supply side and the demand side into account. The (almost) simultaneous publication of the three is often described as the "marginal revolution", as we will explain further below. There are also major differences between the approaches of the three authors, however, which we will explore in chapters 4–6.

At the end of the nineteenth century we find authors such as Alfred Marshall (1842–1924) and John Bates Clark (1847–1938), whose works can be read as syntheses of marginalist economic theory. We will explore their contributions further in chapters 7 and 8. These developments in the later nineteenth century mark the beginning of microeconomics as a separate subfield of economic theory, and the core insights developed by the authors of the marginal revolution are still visible in our contemporary textbooks.

The story above seems to suggest that the history of marginalism is actually equivalent to the history of economic thought, but that would be a very narrow interpretation of the development of the field. Marginalism turned out to be essential for economic methodology, i.e. the way in which economic problems are approached. And as we have said before, the marginal revolution marked the beginning of modern microeconomic theory. But economics is much more than that. The field also studies, among many other things, the effects of different forms of taxation, the adequacy of monetary policy conducted by central banks, and the impact of minimum wage legislation on the unemployment rate. But even in these more applied fields, the influence of the marginalist methodology is prevalent. While we will see some examples in our final chapter, this short book cannot cover all these topics in detail. All attention has been directed to the concepts of "margin" and "marginal", and elaborate discussions of wider matters, though they would be very interesting and important, have been avoided as much as possible. Some interesting extensions that are not essential to the general discussion have been placed in footnotes. A decision has been made to discuss only a relatively limited group of authors, and only those aspects of their works that are directly relevant to the development of "marginalism" have been mentioned. The book is also not meant to be a thoroughly critical history, in order to avoid the pitfall of the history of economic thought that was identified by Kenneth Boulding:

> The student first learned what was wrong with Adam Smith and all the things in which he was wrong and confused, then he went on to learn what was the matter with Ricardo, then what was the matter with John Stuart Mill, and then what was the matter with Marshall. Many students never learned anything that was right at all, and I think emerged from the course with the impression that economics was a monumental collection of errors.   (Boulding 1971: 232)

Instead, we will follow the development of "marginalism" in historical order, and we will allow later authors to criticize and build on the works of their predecessors. No effort has been made to investigate the biographies of our main authors, or to connect their personal backgrounds with the development of their ideas. Many other more substantial histories of economic thought are available that fulfil these purposes.

The first substantial "modern" history of economics is Joseph Schumpeter's *History of Economic Analysis*, first published in 1954. It has been described as a "monumental" and "complete" history of economic thought. It is really an encyclopaedia of substantial length, but it obviously does not cover the important developments in economic theory that occurred after its publication.

Another history of economic thought worth mentioning is Mark Blaug's *Economic Theory in Retrospect*, first published in 1962 but revised several times since, with the latest edition published in 1997. Blaug's book is, however, only suitable for readers who already have a substantial background in modern economic theory. As the book's title states, he considers economic theory in retrospect, which means that he looks at past economic theory from the point of view of the modern economist.

More accessible is Landreth and Colander's *History of Economic Thought* (2002, 4th edition), which I have used as a textbook for my history of economic thought courses. Unfortunately, this book has now gone out of print.

For the reader who is completely unfamiliar with economic theory, Roger Backhouse's *The Ordinary Business of Life: A History of Economics from the Ancient World to the Twenty-First Century* (2002) may be a good general history of economic thought. While it is relatively short, it still provides a coherent overview of the development of economic theory, placed in a broader context.

This little book will focus exclusively on the development of "marginalism". Since marginalism is essentially a theory of valuation, we will first explore how economists prior to 1871 approached the question of "value" of goods and services that are bought and sold in the market place. We will then explore the problems that surrounded these earlier approaches, and the solutions to these problems that were provided by the authors of the marginal revolution. We will also briefly discuss the literature that tried to provide an explanation for the marginal revolution: why did this revolution occur, and why precisely in 1871? We will conclude that there was not really a revolution, but rather a gradual development throughout the nineteenth century. The later chapters of this short history of marginalism will examine the contributions of the different authors in greater detail.

Practical approaches from Aristotle to Petty

What is the "value" of a specific good (or service)? At first sight, the value of a good seems to be equivalent to its market price. However, this market price can fluctuate a lot, due to factors such as bad harvests, wars, increasing or decreasing production costs or changing consumer tastes. Throughout history, economists (and philosophers) have tried to determine the "intrinsic" value of a good, around which the market price fluctuates.

Whereas economists since Adam Smith have tried to address this issue from a theoretical point of view, ancient and medieval philosophers followed a practical or ethical approach. The distinction between theoretical and practical sciences was made by Aristotle (384–322 BCE), the great philosopher who has been described as the founding father of such diverse fields as ethics, logic, biology, physics and economics. Aristotle argues that theoretical sciences investigate eternal truth for its own sake, whereas practical sciences are concerned with the good or bad of human behaviour.[2] Contemporary economists would instead see economics as a theoretical science, as they try to identify the laws that are operational in the economy.

---

2. Aristotle also mentions productive sciences, which aim to create useful or beautiful objects, but these are not relevant to our discussion. More about these matters can be found in Shields (2016).

Some economists would even call economics a positive science that tries to make accurate predictions.[3] Aristotle, however, would see economics as a practical science that describes the rules that need to be followed by the manager of a household. After all, the word *economics* is derived from the Greek words *oikos* (house) and *nomos* (rule, law). Aristotle's approach can be described as normative economics: which rules need to be followed in the management of the household and the farm, given that the good and the just are the ultimate goals to be achieved?

In antiquity, a farm (and therefore a household) being self-sufficient was often seen as ideal. Families should not depend on others for their survival. However, trade was more important in ancient times than is generally thought: goods were exchanged in market places against other goods (using some form of money as a medium of exchange). When analysing these processes of exchange, Aristotle approached the issue from a practical point of view. What is the just price? Are the goods exchanged at a ratio that is "fair" for both parties, or is one person taking advantage of the other? Typically, the two parties engaged in an exchange are unequal and they produce different goods (since otherwise the exchange would make little sense). In his famous example of a shoemaker exchanging shoes for the work of a house builder, he writes that "the number of shoes exchanged for a house ... must therefore correspond to the ratio of builder to shoemaker" (Aristotle 1984: 1788). If the work of the builder (constructing a house) is equivalent to 200 times the work of the shoemaker (making a shoe), then the house will exchange for 200 shoes. Money is only an artificially installed medium of exchange, facilitating the comparison of inherently different goods and services. The "just price" is heavily influenced, if not basically determined, by custom. Injustice appears when, in the act of exchange, one party receives more (and the other therefore less) than "what is equal in accordance with proportion" (Aristotle 1984: 1789). Aristotle's discussion has been interpreted in different ways,[4] but it is clear that his intention was not to set up a theoretical formula to determine the market price of a good, but rather to determine the "just price" using practical investigation.

The same question – what is the just price? – was asked by Thomas Aquinas (1225–74). His purpose is to evaluate the act of exchange: to determine

---

3. See Friedman (1966) for an extensive discussion of economics as a positive science.
4. See, for instance, Soudek (1952).

whether it takes place at a just price, and is therefore morally good or bad. Referring to both Aristotle and biblical sources, Aquinas argues that trading as such is not immoral as long as it is directed towards a virtuous end. A professional trader who is only interested in maximizing profit for its own sake does not act in accordance with justice. It is acceptable for a household farm manager (and occasional trader) to acquire a "moderate gain" by trading in order to support his household, or to be paid for the labour that he delivered to provide some public advantage. It is not morally acceptable, however, to sell a good at a higher price than was paid for it if the good did not undergo any change. If the seller improved the good, or if the value of the good was changed "with the change of place or time", or if there were transportation costs or risks involved, then a higher price is justified (Aquinas 1948: 1510–11). Modern economists would be very dissatisfied with Aquinas's arguments, given that they do not include a precise definition of "value", nor do they lead to a clear determination of a market price. His discourse remains within the realm of practical science, and is directed towards the moral evaluation of an act of exchange.

The emphasis on moral evaluation fades when William Petty (1623–87) uses "political arithmetic" in order to determine the "political anatomy" of Ireland. His "political arithmetic" signifies that he is only willing to express himself "in terms of number, weight or measure; to use only arguments of sense, and to consider only such causes, as have visible foundations in nature" (Petty 1676: 244). The "political anatomy" entails setting up an inventory of Ireland, and estimating the total wealth available in Ireland. Given that products such as butter, cheese, corn and wool are the result of human labour exerted on land, two factors of production need to be considered: labour and land. Suppose that a calf that is put on a piece of land for one year will provide 50 days of food for an average person. These 50 days of food would then represent the value of the land (or the year's rent of the land). Now consider that more could be produced if a man were to exert labour on the same piece of land for a year. Suppose that this would yield 60 days of food for an average person. That surplus of ten days of food would be equal to the wage of that man. It should then be possible to establish "equations" that express the value of all different kinds of goods and resources in terms of numbers of days of food provided for the average person. This should always be the easiest obtainable food in any country, as transportation costs and risks can lead to differences in the regional values.

For instance, the value of an Irish cabin is then worth "the number of days food, which the maker spent in building of it". The same method can be used to value the contribution of technology (or "art") as compared to simple labour. Suppose that 1,000 work days can prepare 100 acres of land for seed. Alternatively, if I were to spend 100 days developing a new invention, then I could prepare 200 acres of land in the remaining 900 days. This would imply that the value of the invention is equal to a man's labour forever, because after the invention one man could produce in the same time what before had to be done by two people. Petty would like to put these methods of valuation into practice. The visible part of people's expense, which is housing, may be used to estimate the "nature of people's feeding", and therefore the value of labour. A similar "equation" would have to be found to establish the value of land, but Petty admits that he is not able "to furnish" one (Petty 1672: 180–3). While it is clear that Petty's economic thought is still an instance of a practical science – he is, after all, setting up an inventory – his considerations are no longer a part of moral discourse. And what is even more interesting is that he paves the way for classical political economy, which would investigate the notion of "value" and the contributions of the different factors of production (such as labour) in a theoretical way.

Classical political economy on value in use and value in exchange

As we have said before, "classical" economists would approach the question of value from a theoretical point of view. Adam Smith, the father of classical political economy,[5] distinguishes between value in use and value in exchange: "The word value, it is to be observed, has two different meanings,

---

5. The term "political economy" refers to the Greek term "polis" or the (city-) state, and therefore signifies the application of "economics" (the rules of management of the household) to the state. Interestingly, the meaning of "management of the state" is reflected in the now rather outmoded Dutch term for economics, *Staathuishoud-kunde*, and in the German term *Volkswirtschaftslehre*. The term "political economy" was exchanged for "economics" by marginalists such as Jevons and Marshall in order to emphasize the scientific status of the field (comparable to subjects such as "physics" and "biology") and to demarcate it from particular political ideologies. As Marshall (1890: 43) states: "But it [economics] shuns many political issues, which the practical man cannot ignore: and it is therefore a science, pure and applied, rather than a science and an art. And it is better described by the broad term 'Economics' than by the narrower term 'Political Economy'."

and sometimes expresses the utility of some particular object, and sometimes the power of purchasing other goods which the possession of that object conveys" (Smith 1776: 31). For instance, water is extremely useful but it can be bought at a low market price: it has a high value in use but a low value in exchange. A diamond, by contrast, has a low value in use but a very high value in exchange. There seems to be no clear relationship between a good's value in use and its value in exchange. The exchange value of a good (in terms of other goods) or its market price (in terms of money) consists of several components.

Consider a primitive nation of hunters, where killing a beaver requires twice as much labour as killing a deer. In such a simple society, the beaver will be sold on the market for twice the price of a deer: the market price of a good is directly proportional to the amount of labour needed to acquire it. In this primitive hunting society, land is freely available, and there is no capital. There are no farmers and no manufacturers. When this society develops, farmers and subsequently manufacturers will employ labourers to produce goods for the market. As a result, capital will be accumulated in the hands of a few manufacturers.

Capital is a difficult concept, which has different meanings for different economists, as we will see later on. In the first instance we can see capital as tools, and raw materials, that are owned by the manufacturer and that are advanced to the labourers. But the labourers also need to survive during the production process, before the final products have been sold at the market. They will therefore also receive subsistence (in the form of wages) from the manufacturer, which will allow them to survive and to raise a family. The manufacturer will thus provide labourers with materials as well as with subsistence, or wages, and these payments come from his capital stock. These manufacturers will require remuneration for the use of their capital stock (used to assist and feed the labourers), and this is their profit. In any particular place, this profit is usually a fixed percentage of the stock, e.g. ten per cent.

Furthermore, at some point in the development of our society, all available land will have become private property. The landlords will then also demand payment for the use of the soil they own, which becomes rent. The market price of any good in a more advanced society therefore resolves itself into three components: wages of labour, profits of stock and rent of land

(Smith 1776: 53–61). Interest is the payment for the use of money, which is actually a derivative of the profit of stock: the manufacturer borrows money from the lender and pays compensation, which comes from his profit.

The profit rate tends to be equal in different sectors in a given society, since manufacturers may withdraw their capital from a sector with a lower profit rate and invest it instead in a sector with a higher profit rate. Given this movement of capital, the supply of goods will decrease in the former sector and increase in the latter. As we know from the so-called law of supply and demand, if the supply of a certain good increases, then the suppliers will compete with each other to find the buyers, and therefore they will lower the price. A lower price is also required to sell all goods, since demand is assumed to remain unchanged. It follows that the market price in the sector with the initially higher profit rate will go down (since supply goes up), whereas in the sector with the initially lower profit rate the market price will go up (since supply goes down). These price changes will equalize the profit rates. This is the famous "invisible hand" mechanism, which tends to equalize profit rates in a society because of competition between manufacturers.[6] Smith distinguishes further between the market price and the natural price of a good: "The natural price, therefore, is, as it were, the central price, to which the prices of all commodities are continually gravitating" (Smith 1776: 65). Modern economists would prefer to speak about the long-term price, around which the short-term market price fluctuates, due to occasional and temporary fluctuations in demand or supply.[7]

Ricardo elaborates on Smith's definitions of value, but he remarks that value in use is a prerequisite for value in exchange. If a good has no utility, then nobody wants it and therefore it will have no value in exchange. Given that a good has utility, it derives its value in exchange from its scarcity and from the quantity of labour required to obtain it. Ricardo excludes certain

---

6. The phrase "invisible hand" is usually connected with Adam Smith, but note that he uses the "invisible hand" expression only once in his *Wealth of Nations* (Smith 1776: 485).

7. Marshall writes that the normal or "natural" value of a commodity according to Adam Smith "is that which economic forces tend to bring about *in the long run*. It is the average value which economic forces would bring about if the general conditions of life were stationary for a run of time long enough to enable them all to work out their full effect" (Marshall 1890: 163).

goods from his analysis: namely, rare and scarce objects such as works of art, the supply of which cannot be increased by the exertion of labour. Repeating Smith's example of the primitive hunting society, he agrees that the foundation of the exchange value of a good is the amount of labour required to produce that good. There is, however, a difference between the quantity of labour bestowed on a good and the quantity of labour that the good would purchase on the market (i.e. other goods on which labour was bestowed). The first is usually invariable but the second tends to fluctuate a lot. It is not the amount of labour bestowed on the good per se that determines the value, it is rather the relative proportions of labour required to produce two different goods that will determine their relative rate of exchange. This is as it is in Smith's example of the primitive society: since it takes twice as much time to kill a beaver as to kill a deer, the price of the beaver will be twice the price of a deer. However, Ricardo notes that there are different qualities of labour: a day's work of a jewellery manufacturer may be worth more than a day's work of a common labourer. It is therefore not simply quantity of labour that needs to be taken into account, but also the comparative skill and intensity of that labour.

As Smith remarked, a more advanced society will also use capital as a factor of production. If the cost of labour, i.e. the wages, increases, then the price of goods produced in labour-intensive industries (such as agriculture) will increase more than the price of goods produced in capital-intensive industries (such as manufacturing). Ricardo also understands that the length of time of the production process is a consideration: if the capital needs to remain invested for a year, then more profit will be required compared with a situation in which the capital only needs to remain invested for a month. Ricardo does not, however, make precise calculations about these matters. Using some numerical examples he concludes that the change in the relative price of goods, following a change in the wage rate (which affects different sectors differently, depending on how relatively labour intensive they are), can only account for minor deviations between rates of profits in different sectors.[8] The relative market prices of goods are therefore (almost entirely) to be explained by the relative amounts of labour required to produce those goods.

---

8. Ricardo's numerical example shows a deviation of 6 or 7 per cent, which made Stigler (1958) write about Ricardo's 93 per cent labour theory of value.

Profits can only increase when wages, which Ricardo calls the value of labour, go down (Ricardo 1817: 17–44):

> The rate of profits is never increased by a better distribution of labour, by the invention of machinery, by the establishment of roads and canals, or by any means of abridging labour either in the manufacture or in the conveyance of goods. These are causes which operate on price … but they have no effect whatever on profit.
>
> (Ricardo 1817: 93)

If, due to technological progress, shoes can now be produced with 20 per cent less labour than before (everything else remaining the same), then the relative market price of shoes will simply fall by 20 per cent. Profits will not be affected by this technological advance.

We will see in the next chapter that the rental price of land does not enter into the market price as it is reduced to zero for goods that are produced in the least favourable circumstances. For the determination of wages in classical political economy, we need to bring in the theory of population, which was presented by Ricardo's critical contemporary and friend Malthus.

Malthus tried to find a solution for an apparent contradiction in society, where on the one hand there is enlightenment and scientific progress, but on the other hand there is great suffering in the growing population, especially among the poorer classes. His argumentation starts with two simple facts of life that cannot possibly be denied: that food is necessary for human existence, and that "the passion between the sexes" is required for the survival of humanity. In the United States of the early nineteenth century these two facts did not lead to severe distress: there was sufficient food available and the "manners" of the population were "pure", which implies that there were no checks to early marriages.

As observed in the United States (by Malthus), the implication is that the population will double every 25 years. In England, where all the fertile land had already been taken into cultivation, this was a serious problem. The English population was also growing quickly but agricultural production could not keep up. Malthus illustrates his argument with a simple numerical example. Whereas population grows in a geometrical ratio (1, 2, 4, 8, 16, 32, etc.), food production can only grow in an arithmetical ratio (1, 2, 3, 4, 5, 6, etc.).[9] An increase in population growth will increase the demand for food and will therefore lead to an increase in food prices, because food production cannot increase at the same pace. This will inevitably lead to food shortages, which will first and foremost affect the weakest parts of the population (the poor, and also the ill, the elderly and children).[10] Since there are more labourers than employers, there will be more competition between them, and the employers will be able to lower *nominal wages* (which are also called money wages, e.g. €10 per hour). Not only will nominal wages be lower, but the purchasing power of the population will decrease further because of rising food prices. *Real wages* (expressed in terms of purchasing power, e.g. 3kg of potatoes for one hour of labour) will therefore further decrease. For instance, where before a labourer could purchase 4kg of potatoes with €10, he may now only receive €9 and be able to purchase only 3kg of potatoes. The real wage has gone down for two reasons: the hourly nominal wage decreased from €10 to €9 and the price of potatoes increased from €2.50 to €3.00 per kg. These tendencies will result in famines, diseases and fewer marriages, which will eventually decrease the population. And this will in turn reverse the entire process: population will decrease, demand for food will decrease, food prices will decline, and unemployment will go down again (given the decreasing population). Both nominal and real wages will increase again. But given the inevitable truth of Malthus's two facts of life, at some point the process will again be reversed, and the population will continuously "oscillate" between periods of relative prosperity and periods of serious distress (Malthus 1798: 67–80).

All this implies that real wages will, on average, be at subsistence level: if people earn more than they strictly need to survive, the population will grow; if people earn less than subsistence, the population will decrease. The

---

9. The modern reader, who is familiar with butter mountains and milk lakes, should keep in mind that labour productivity in agriculture was very low in the nineteenth century, and that a large part of the population was (still) working in agriculture. But the ultimate reason why food production cannot be thought to grow in more than an arithmetical ratio is the limited availability of fertile land (which is, especially in the absence of modern techniques, a substantial problem). There were also many famines in the nineteenth century, and the provision of food has been a major problem for the economists of that time.

10. See Vorzimmer (1969) for a discussion of Malthus's influence on Darwin's theory of natural selection.

conclusion is that, in the classical system, the "natural" wage is equal to the subsistence wage: that that is just sufficient to survive. Ricardo's statement that profits can only rise when wages decrease now becomes clear: given that wages are at subsistence level, they can only decrease when the price of food (and necessities) goes down, because of technological progress in agriculture and food processing or by the importation of cheap foreign food and necessities consumed by the labouring population.[11] Note that Ricardo does not regard this subsistence level as a biological minimum, given that it is determined by habit and custom (Ricardo 1817: 67–8).

John Stuart Mill, the greatest English classical political economist, concludes that "there is nothing in the laws of value which remains for the present or any future writer to clear up; the theory of the subject is complete" (Mill 1848: 436). However, he claimed the concepts needed to be clarified: "value" in economics is actually "value in exchange", which is a relative term. There is also a clear difference between "value" and "price": "value" refers to the purchasing power of a good in terms of other goods, whereas "price" expresses the value of a thing in relation to money. Modern economists would talk about real versus nominal. Mill states that a good can only have value (in exchange) if it is useful and if there is some difficulty in its attainment. Value (and therefore price) then depends on the ratio between effectual demand and supply, where "effectual" demand denotes not simply the desire for a good, since it must be combined with the power of purchasing: a beggar may desire a diamond, but given his poverty this desire will never translate into a real purchase and will therefore not influence the price.

However, demand and supply will only govern the value of goods that cannot be increased indefinitely. For all other goods, which can be reproduced indefinitely, demand and supply can only lead to "perturbations of value", since value will always gravitate to the cost of production. If the value were to fall below the cost of production, then nobody would be

---

11. Note that this only works for goods that are consumed by the labourers. If the price of luxury goods decreases because of technological progress or cheaper imports, then the price of these luxury goods will go down. Consumers of luxury goods will be able to purchase more units of the luxury good for the same sum of money, but the profit rate will not be affected. Profits can only increase when wages go down, and given that wages are at subsistence level, wages can only go down when the prices of wage goods decrease.

willing to produce the good and capital would be withdrawn from this sector; less will be produced in this sector and the price would go up. If the value rises above the cost of production, then increased profits would attract more capital to the sector; more will be produced and the price will go down.

The cost of production includes wages, but not the quantity of labour. Another element of the cost of production is profit, which is the return for abstinence: rather than consuming his capital directly, the capitalist purchases machinery and advances subsistence to the labourers. As Mill puts it, "The natural value of some things is a scarcity value; but most things naturally exchange for one another in the ratio of their cost of production, or what may be termed their cost value" (Mill 1848: 478). Mill therefore clarifies Smith's notion of "natural value" in terms of cost of production by referring to the invisible hand mechanism.

Karl Marx on value and surplus value

Not all economists agreed with Mill's clarification. Karl Marx (1818–83) turns Ricardian economic theory into a labour theory of value, and develops a theory of value and surplus value. He revisits the distinction between use value, which he describes as qualitative, and exchange value, which he sees as something quantitative. The use value of a good stems from its utility, which in turn depends on the physical properties of the good. As an example, the use value of a shoe consists of protecting a human foot. This use value will only surface in the act of consumption, and it is disregarded in the act of exchange: by exchanging one good against another, we give up the possibility to consume the good, and therefore its use value. An exchange of goods can be represented with an equation, which expresses that a certain quantity of a good is equated with a certain quantity of another. Given that this equation holds, there must be a third thing, different from the two goods, to which these goods can be reduced. As Marx put it, "If then we leave out of consideration the use value of commodities, they have only one common property left, that of being products of labour" (Marx 1867: 48). However, in the act of exchange we ignore not only the useful qualities of the good, but also the useful characteristics of the various kinds of labour. The third thing required to make two (or more) different goods comparable in the act of exchange is, therefore, human labour in the abstract (or labour in general). A good has more value than another because more abstract human labour is required for its production.

Given that the value of a good does not depend on whether it was made by a lazy and inefficient person or by an efficient worker, we need to take the average at the societal level to find this abstract human labour. This is socially necessary labour, taken on the average, which depends on the level of technological development prevailing in a society: the average labourer can produce a good more quickly in a modern, technological society compared with a worker living in the stone age, for instance. "We see then that that which determines the magnitude of the value of any article is the amount of labour socially necessary, or the labour time socially necessary for its production" (Marx 1867: 49). This implies that goods that are not the result of human labour, such as air or virgin soil, cannot have value, even though they are useful. On the other hand, a good cannot have any value if it is useless, as the labour embodied in it would be useless as well, and therefore cannot be counted as labour since it does not create any value (Marx 1867: 45–51).[12]

All these considerations are irrelevant for an individual who lives on his own and simply consumes the products of his own labour. Daniel Defoe's *Robinson Crusoe*, who lived alone on an island (before the arrival of Friday), is often cited as an example by economists. However, in an advanced state of society, production takes place at the societal level, and besides the labourer there is the capitalist, who owns the means of production, such as buildings, machines and tools. According to Marx the labourer produces for the capitalist, and therefore she produces not only value but also surplus value, which the capitalist turns into profit. The labourer produces more than simply the subsistence amount, which she receives as wages, and the rest is appropriated by the capitalist.

The capitalist would like to increase the amount of surplus value, and this can be accomplished in two different ways. First, the working day can be extended: the labourer works longer hours but receives the same remuneration as before. Marx calls this the production of absolute surplus value. Second, the necessary labour to produce the good can be reduced,

---

12. Marx's approach has been heavily criticized by, for example, Eugen von Böhm-Bawerk (1884: 367–92).

which basically means that the wage goods, which the labourer receives as compensation for her work, are earned in less time. This is the production of relative surplus value, which corresponds to Ricardo's argument that profits can only rise when wages fall, and therefore by making wage goods cheaper (by technological progress in the wage goods industry or through the importation of cheaper foreign wage goods). However, Marx disagrees with Ricardo when the latter states that the labourer receives the value of her labour, namely her wages, as compensation. Labourers only receive the cost of their labour as (subsistence) wages, and the surplus value is appropriated by the capitalist. Ricardo's analysis therefore conceals the origin of surplus value (Marx 1867: 509–19).

The marginal revolution

So far we have summarized the development of value theory that preceded the marginal revolution of 1871. The natural value of a good is essentially determined by its cost of production, which includes profits and wages. The market price fluctuates around this natural value, thanks to the operation of the "invisible hand". The invisible hand also ensures that profit rates are equalized across different sectors of the economy. The Malthusian population theory implies that wages are at subsistence level. Whereas Mill argued that the laws of value have been fully clarified, Marx criticized classical political economy for concealing the power relation between the capitalists, who own all the capital, and the labourers, who are forced to sell their labour at subsistence cost since they do not own any capital.

Jevons, who did not know the writings of Marx, was also critical of classical political economy:

> I believe it is generally supposed that Adam Smith laid the foundations of this science; that Malthus, Anderson and Senior added important doctrines; that Ricardo systematised the whole; and, finally, that Mr. J. S. Mill filled in the details and completely expounded this branch of knowledge. (Jevons 1871: v)

In his *Theory of Political Economy* (1871), Jevons attempts to treat economics as "a calculus of pleasures and pains", and sketches out the new form of the science "almost irrespective of previous opinions". He argues that the introduction of mathematical science into economics, and especially calculus, gives rise to the establishment of accurate quantitative notions of previously ill-defined economic concepts such as value, utility, labour, capital and so forth (Jevons 1871: vi–viii).

This apparent radical break with tradition is remarkable, especially since the French author Walras expressed a similar "revolutionary attitude" in his *Elements of Pure Economics* (1874):

> the publication of an elementary treatise in political and social economics, distributed following a novel plan, elaborated according to an original method, of which the conclusions, I have to say, will also differ, in certain points, from those of the actual science.
> (Walras 1874: 1; my translation)[13]

Walras writes that he became acquainted with Jevons's work only one month before his *Elements* was published, and that it certainly did not have any influence on the preparation of his own manuscript. Walras emphasizes the similarities between his *Elements* and Jevons's *Theory*: they both use mathematics, especially in the theory of exchange; and Jevons's exchange equation is identical to Walras's condition of "maximum satisfaction" (which we will explore in later chapters).

Also in 1871, the Austrian economist Menger published his *Grundsätze der Volkswirtschaftslehre* without knowing either Jevons or Walras or their works. This work is, however, fundamentally different, as it does not contain any mathematical formalism. Moreover, he is somewhat less revolutionary, as he recognizes the existence of (mainly German) predecessors, but his intention was, nevertheless, to undertake a "reform":

> It was a special joy to us that the field that we are working on, including its most general teachings, has been to a considerable extent the intellectual property of the newest developments in German political economy, and that our attempted reform of the highest principles of our science has therefore been built on the

---

13. "… la publication d'un traité élémentaire d'économie politique et sociale distribué suivant un plan nouveau, élaboré d'après une méthode originale, et dont les conclusions, je dois le dire, différeront aussi, sur certains points, de celles de la science actuelle.".

foundations laid by preparatory work, which almost exclusively has been created by German academic industriousness.

(Menger 1871: x; my translation)[14]

Problems for classical political economy

To a greater or lesser extent, the three authors of the marginal revolution wanted to reform the discipline of economics. This suggests that there were some fundamental difficulties with classical political economy in general, and with the attempt to use a cost of production theory of value in order to determine market prices in particular. These difficulties are intertwined with some concerns about the distribution of the final product: which part goes to wages and which part goes to profits? This can be explained as follows. When a product is sold at the market, an income is generated. Part of this income will be paid to workers as wages, and another part will be paid to manufacturers (or capitalists) as profits. Since wages and profits are part of cost of production, and cost of production is said to determine value, it follows that the classical system also needs to determine the share that goes to wages and profits. Otherwise, the reasoning would be circular. If the value of a good is determined by its cost of production, which mainly consists of wages, then a good will be more valuable, and therefore its market price higher, when more wages are required to generate the good. However, a wage is also a price: namely, the price for a specific form of labour. Therefore, one set of prices (namely, wages) is used to explain another set of prices (see Landreth & Colander 2002: 96–7).

The cost of production approach therefore presupposes that the wage rate can be determined beforehand. As we have seen, the classical economists maintained a natural wage rate, which is equal to the subsistence level. If the actual wage rate exceeds this natural rate, then the population grows; if

---

14. "Eine besondere Freude war es uns, dass das hier von uns bearbeitete, die allgemeinsten Lehren unserer Wissenschaft umfassende Gebiet zum nicht geringen Theile so recht eigentlich das Besitzthum der neueren Entwickelungen der deutschen National-Oekonomie ist und die hier versuchte Reform der höchsten Principien unserer Wissenschaft demnach auf der Grundlage von Vorarbeiten erfolgt, welche fast ausnahmslos deutscher Forscherfleiss geschaffen hat."

it were below the natural rate, then the population would decrease. Hence, the Malthusian population theory explains why wages are at subsistence level. It is true that real wages were fairly low and real income growth was at best moderate in the nineteenth century.[15] However, we also know that the Malthusian population theory does not work for more advanced countries. Growing wealth and higher incomes do not automatically lead to a growth in population, as wealthier families may decide to have fewer rather than more children. As we will see in our next chapter, the Irish economist Mountifort Longfield (1834) had already recognized that, in prosperous times, wages could rise above the subsistence level. Marx also disagreed with the Malthusian population theory, as it explains the "over-population" by referring to a natural law, whereas it should be explained by the laws of capitalist development (Marx 1867: 529). When wages increase, capitalists will replace labourers by machines, which will reproduce the "industrial reserve army", i.e. the amount of unemployed workers looking for a job. This will decrease their bargaining power and therefore lower the wage rate. The classical conclusion that wages are at subsistence level is therefore maintained, but the explanation is provided by a social law, relative to capitalism.

Nevertheless, even marginalist authors such as Jevons and Marshall did not completely write off the Malthusian theory of population, but they no longer used it as a cornerstone in their theories of value. According to Mark Blaug (1962: 281), classical political economy relied on a "depart-mentalised approach": land rent was explained as a differential surplus (see the next chapter); wages were at subsistence level, and were therefore governed by the long-term production costs of means of subsistence; and profits were treated as a residual, i.e. they consisted of what was left after wages (and land rent) were paid. The authors of the marginal revolution wanted to set up a universal theory that would treat land, labour and capital simply as factors of production that would be rewarded following the same principles. The amount paid to each factor of production would be determined by its scarcity, in relation to consumers' wants for the products that these factors could produce. This implies that consumer demand, and therefore utility, received a more prominent place in economic theory.

---

15. Crafts and Mills (1994) use modern time series analysis to conclude that the trend rate of growth was zero for the period 1750–1813 and about 1.2 per cent per year for the period 1813–1913.

Whereas classical economics was more focused on production and supply, marginalist economics shifted the emphasis in the direction of utility and demand. The central problem for economics was to maximize consumers' utility, by allocating scarce resources such as land, labour and capital in the most optimal way.

Another major, though related, difference between classical and marginalist economics is the relationship between exchange and distribution (Dobb 1973: 167–77). Exchange is concerned with the determination of the market price, which generates income when the product is sold. Distribution is concerned with the determination of the income share that goes to the different holders of the factors of production (such as land, labour and capital). For the classical economists, distribution was regarded as prior to exchange. This means that they would consider which part of the produce would be distributed to the different classes of society first, before going on to consider the market price. Given the natural value of a product, which was based on its cost of production, it could be determined which income share would go to wages and which share to profits even before the product was brought to the market. The market price might fluctuate around this natural value, but on average and in the long run they would be equal. The market price was therefore not needed to determine income shares.

Marginalist economics, by contrast, reduced the problem of distribution to a problem of pricing. While the classical economists looked at distribution from an aggregate point of view – which part of the value of the final products goes to wages and to profits in general – the marginalists took individual producers and consumers, not social classes, as the starting point for their analysis. The economy was depicted as an interconnected system of inputs and outputs that are determined simultaneously. Such a system can only be set up using mathematical techniques, particularly calculus. Earlier economists such as Smith and Ricardo used quantities and numerical examples but did not rely on mathematics. As we explore further in chapter 4, Jevons argued that mathematics (and calculus in particular) provided an adequate language to be used by economists. Walras went even further than Jevons when he argued that the entire economy could be represented by a set of equations, which would be determined simultaneously. We examine Walras's "general equilibrium theory" further in chapter 5. Note, however, that not all marginalists were in favour of the use of mathematics: as we discuss in chapter 6, the Austrian School of Carl Menger is a notable exception in this respect.

Possible explanations for the marginal revolution

It seems remarkable that, around more or less the same time, three different authors, who came from different backgrounds, independently developed the central principles of marginalist economic theory:

> The term "marginal revolution" is usually taken to refer to the nearly simultaneous but completely independent discovery in the early 1870s by Jevons, Menger and Walras of the principle of diminishing marginal utility as the fundamental building block of a new kind of static microeconomics.   (Blaug 1972: 269)

Numerous historians of economic thought have examined this phenomenon.[16] Blaug (1962: 282–7) lists four possible explanations for the marginal revolution: an autonomous intellectual development; the product of philosophical currents; the product of institutional changes in the economy; and an attempt to contradict Marxist economic theory. None of these explanations appear to be satisfactory.

---

16. Heimann (1945) emphasizes the similarity between the three different authors, since they all relied on utility value. Paul (1979) describes the struggle of several classical theories with analytical and/or practical problems, which the authors of the marginal revolution tried to solve. Hutchison (1978) argues that the problems of British classical political economy may explain the emergence of Jevons's marginalist economics but that a similar explanation cannot be given for Walras and Menger, who worked in harmony with prevailing ideas. Dobb (1973: 167–77) describes the shift in attention from production costs to demand and final consumption, and the shift from regarding distribution as prior to exchange to an interconnected system of inputs and outputs that are determined simultaneously. Dobb also argues that insights into larger macroeconomic relations were excluded or neglected after the marginal revolution, which implies that the ideological implications were not incidental. Winch (1972: 432) relates the shift in emphasis to a closer attention to what is knowable by deductive theory. Deane (1978: 106) argues that the attention shifted from the search for the meaning of value to determinants of market price.

The "autonomous intellectual development" explanation has some merits when looking at the British case, since Jevons did react against earlier classical authors and was inspired by other British authors (such as Bentham, Jennings and MacLeod).[17] But this explanation cannot be applied to the Continent. Walras and Menger did not react against an older prevailing tradition, but developed their ideas in line with earlier French and German authors. And even if we only consider the British case, the thesis of an "autonomous intellectual development" is unsatisfactory because it does not explain why the revolution occurred in 1871–74. Why not earlier or later?

This implies that some changes in context need to be identified, but "philosophical currents" do not provide an accurate explanation for the marginal revolution either. The philosophical systems of British empiricism and hedonism, French rationalism and German idealism differ radically from each other. Furthermore, although Jevons was certainly inspired by Bentham's moral theory of utilitarianism (see chapter 4), Walras was not interested in philosophy and there is no evidence that Menger was motivated by the study of a specific philosophical system.

The explanation that points to "institutional changes in the economy" is unsatisfactory for similar reasons: the economic contexts of Britain and the Continent were quite different, and it is difficult for historians of economic thought to make the personal intellectual awareness of these institutional changes visible in the writings of our main authors.

Finally, the "attempt to contradict Marxist economic theory" is also unconvincing as a possible explanation. Later marginalists (such as the Austrian economist Eugen von Böhm-Bawerk) did use marginalist theory to contradict the labour theory of value as developed by Marx, but Jevons, Walras and Menger did not know Marx's writings when they wrote their books. Moreover, it is also clear that at least Jevons and Walras were not simply pro-capitalist writers who wanted to suppress labourers, as there are important social aspects in their works.[18]

Since it appears to be difficult to explain why our three authors came up with similar ideas around the same time, the question of whether their ideas were really that similar arises. It is true that our three main authors maintain two external determinants of value – scarcity and utility – but

---

17. See Mosselmans (2007) for a description of Jevons's attempt to reconstruct economics.
18. See Jolink (1996) for a broader view of Walras's works, and Bowman (1987) and Mosselmans (2007) on the social aspects of Jevons's works.

their intentions and basic attitudes differ fundamentally. This was explored by Jaffé (1976), who argued that Jevons, Walras and Menger should become "de-homogenised". For instance, the notion of "marginal utility" is used differently by our three authors:

> Jevons started out from Bentham's felicific calculus; I don't believe I have seen Bentham's name mentioned once in all of Walras' writings, published or unpublished, which is not surprising since he had always exhibited a strong antipathy to "utilitarisme". Jevons focused his attention from the beginning on what Edgeworth called "Hedinometry" and bestowed concentrated effort on an attempt to reduce utilitarian speculations to an exact science which would be useful as a foundation for the theory of value in exchange; while Walras peremptorily and nonchalantly – too nonchalantly some would say – postulated a measurable marginal utility theory without more ado, for the sole purpose of rounding out his previously formulated catallactic theory of price determination.
>
> (Jaffé 1976: 518)

In other words, Jevons built his work around the notion of "marginal utility" (which he called "final degree of utility"), whereas Walras developed his mathematical theory, which represented the entire economy as a set of equations, before he became acquainted with a marginal utility notion of value (which he needed to relate utility to demand, as we will discuss in chapter 5). According to Streissler (1972: 426–7), the marginalist notions were not central at all to the Austrian school of economics, of which Menger can be considered the founder. "Marginal utility" (which Menger called "*Grenznutzen*") was introduced in the middle of Menger's *Grundsätze*, but it is not a keystone of his theory.

Further differences between our three authors can be identified. We already indicated that mathematics was of little use to Menger, as he communicated to Walras in 1883 (Jaffé 1978: 518–22). By contrast, Jevons and Walras wanted to reconstruct economic theory using the language of mathematics. But while Walras constructed a general equilibrium theory, which represented the economy as a set of equations to describe a system of interconnected markets, Jevons did not pay much attention to interactions between markets and could not derive multiple equilibrium prices from his system (Jaffé 1978: 511–8). Menger was not even interested in equilibrium prices at all, let alone in the formulation of a system of general equilibrium. He was more interested in the underlying (psychological) forces at work in the complex appearance of the social economy. Where Jevons and Walras depict mechanically acting economic agents, who are using reason to maximize utility and profits, Menger has uncertainty, fear and imperfect information at the core of his theory.

The differences between Jevons, Walras and Menger are therefore substantial. Moreover, as we will examine in the next two chapters, the main ideas of "marginalism" were already formulated well before 1871. In his introductory article to the 1972 special volume of *History of Political Economy* on the marginal revolution, Blaug concludes that it was a process, not an event; that there was no multiple discovery, but only temporal coincidence of several singletons;[19] and that "the success of the marginal revolution is intimately associated with the professionalization of economics in the last quarter of the nineteenth century, and it is this which constitutes the problem that must be, and to some extent has been, explained by historians of economic thought" (Blaug 1972: 280).

That the development of marginalism was not really a revolution but rather a slow process can already be inferred from the slow acceptance of the concept of "marginalism", as Howey (1972: 280–3) demonstrates. Hobson used the word in 1914 to denote the acceptance of economists of both marginal utility and marginal productivity. In 1930, the *Handwörterbuch der Staatswissenschaften* contained only one reference under the heading of "Marginalismus" (a reference to Hobson), and the word "marginalism" occurred only seldom in the *Encyclopaedia of the Social Sciences* (1930–35). In 1966 the word entered an English dictionary for the first time. The slow pace of acceptance of "marginalism" can also be traced in the development of American textbooks of economics. From 1893 to 1907, marginal utility entered most textbooks, but marginal productivity remained absent until 1908. In 1934, Hicks and Allen introduced the "marginal rate of substitution" (see chapter 8), and "marginal utility" lost favour. Chamberlin and Robinson made extensive use of "marginal cost" and "marginal revenue", and Keynes's

---

19. The term "multiple discovery" is typically associated with the sociologist Robert Merton (1910–2003), who researched multiple independent discoveries in the history of science, i.e. the simultaneous discovery of the same theories or inventions by different people, independent of each other, and around the same time (several singletons).

General Theory contained the use of marginal terms as constants (again see chapter 8). These improvements entered the textbooks between 1937 and 1947. Samuelson's famous textbook appeared for the first time in 1948 and provided the new standard. In 1970, the new edition devoted twice as much space to marginalism as did the original edition (Howey 1972: 280–3).

This slow process was accompanied by a growing professionalization of the discipline. Schumpeter (1954: 754–7) argues that the the "revolution" of 1871 was followed by at least two decades of struggle, which was accompanied by professionalization. New organizations were established, e.g. the Verein für Sozialpolitik (1872), the American Economic Association (1885) and the Royal Economic Society (1890). The yearly meetings of the American Economic Association allowed large-scale teamwork for the first time. New economics journals (e.g. the *Quarterly Journal of Economics* and the *Economic Journal*) and new dictionaries and encyclopedias (*The Palgrave Dictionary of Political Economy*) came into existence.

The late nineteenth century is also the period in which separate faculties of economics were founded at universities, where economics had previously been a (small) department attached to the faculty of law or the faculty of arts and humanities. Schumpeter (1954: 754) remarks that the "professionalization" of economics may be seen as "professocialization" as well: the use of improved mathematical techniques implied that economic theory became less accessible to a general public. We can conclude that the (slow) development of marginalism coincided with the development of the field of economics into a separate domain, with its own (mathematical) language, taught in separate faculties of economics and published in separate journals of economics.

The result was a completely different view of what economics is and should do. Adam Smith investigated the "wealth of nations" and tried to find means to improve this wealth:

> After 1870, however, economists typically posited some given supply of productive factors, determined independently by elements outside the purview of analysis. The essence of the economic problem was to search for the conditions under which given productive services were allocated with optimal results among competing uses, optimal in the sense of maximising consumers' satisfactions. This ruled out consideration of the effects of increases in the quantity

and quality of resources and the dynamic expansion of wants, effects that the classical economists had regarded as the sine qua non of improvements in economic welfare. For the first time, economics truly became the science that studies the relationship between given ends and given scarce means that have alternative uses for the achievement of those ends. The classical theory of economic development was replaced by the concept of general equilibrium within an essentially static framework.   (Blaug 1962: 278)

Overview of the book

We have argued above that the key ideas of "marginalism" were already formulated before 1871. Many predecessors of the marginal revolution can be identified, some of which are rather focused on the supply side of the economy whereas others direct attention to the demand side. Chapter 2 elaborates further on the supply side, and devotes specific attention to the theory of rent, which explains how landowners derive income from the possession of fertile land. This theory of rent is obviously of the utmost relevance for a mainly agricultural society, but it will also evolve into a general paradigm for marginalist economic theory. We will specifically consider David Ricardo's theory of rent, Samuel Longfield's discussion of diminishing marginal returns, and Johann Heinrich von Thünen's application of calculus to economic problems.

Chapter 3 then continues with the development of marginalism on the demand side of the economy. Here we will find the academic outsider Hermann Heinrich Gossen, who developed the theory of diminishing marginal utility, which came to be known as Gossen's first law. We also mention Charles Dupuit, whose contribution connected the notion of utility with demand.

The next chapters discuss the contributions of the main authors of the marginal revolution. Chapter 4 is devoted to the work of William Stanley Jevons, which is very similar to Gossen's but starts from a utilitarian perspective (i.e. the ethical theory developed by Jeremy Bentham). His "law of indifference", currently known as the "law of one price" (that a good must be sold at the same price in the market), turns out to be essential for marginalism. Furthermore, Jevons indicates that the theory of rent could be extended to a general theory of (mathematical) economics, but he did not fully work out the consequences of this insight. Jevons's discussion is also restricted to simple cases, such as an exchange economy with only two "trading bodies" and two goods.

In chapter 5 we meet Léon Walras, who developed a general equilibrium theory: a mathematical model that takes all sectors of the economy and their mutual interactions into account. His mathematical approach was inspired by the work of the French scientist Antoine Augustin Cournot (1838). General equilibrium theory implies that supply and demand in every market are equal to each other, which allows us to derive equilibrium prices and quantities for all goods that are being exchanged in the entire economy.

Chapter 6 presents a discussion of the contribution of the Austrian school to marginalism and investigates the works of Carl Menger and Friedrich von Wieser. Their subjective approach focuses strongly on the relevant (decision) processes, rather than on equilibrium outcomes. The works of Menger and Wieser deviate significantly from the writings of both Jevons and Walras, as they do not use mathematics and do not presuppose the existence of perfect knowledge.

In chapter 7 we investigate the contributions of the later nineteenth century, made by Alfred Marshall and John Bates Clark, which can be seen as a synthesis of marginalist theory. Marshall uses the concept of "time" to resolve the problems surrounding the relationship between value, cost and utility, and he introduces (among many other things) the important notion of "consumer surplus". Clark turns the theory of rent into a general theory of income distribution, with marginalism at the core of his analysis.

Our final chapter (chapter 8) then explores some extensions and applications of marginalism in the twentieth century, including the origin of welfare analysis (Pigou), the development of industrial economics and industrial organization (Marshall, Robinson, Chamberlin), the emergence of the "marginal rate of (technical) substitution" (Hicks and Allen), and the application of marginalist principles in macroeconomics (Keynes).

2

Supply-side marginalism: Ricardo and the theory of rent

The development of marginalism on the supply side (namely, the production of goods) is often associated with the theory of rent, which is paid to landlords for the use of their fertile land. In the last chapter, we mentioned that the theory of rent is a cornerstone of classical political economy. While several authors (such as Anderson, Torrens, West and Malthus) have been named as founders of this theory, the best-known version is associated with David Ricardo. In what follows, first we describe Ricardo's theory of rent, in which the idea of diminishing returns appears. There are diminishing returns in agriculture, because fertile land is not available in an unlimited quantity. We then go on to investigate Samuel Mountifort Longfield's *Lectures on Political Economy Delivered in Trinity and Michaelmas Terms*, in which he elaborates on diminishing returns in agriculture and extends the theory to diminishing returns in manufacturing. Finally, we will investigate the *Isolated State* of Johann Heinrich von Thünen, who applies mathematics, and in particular differential calculus, to discuss the notion of diminishing returns.

Ricardo's principles of political economy

In Ricardo's society, landlords, who own fertile land, are an important social class. Their land is rented by farmers, who use their own labour (and the labour of their families) to farm the land to produce agricultural goods. According to Ricardo (1817: 45), "rent is that portion of the produce of the earth which is paid to the landlord for the use of the original and indestructible powers of the soil". Let us suppose that a farmer can produce

100 kilogrammes of corn on a given piece of land (within a year), and that he has to pay 20 kilogrammes of corn to the owner of the land as rent. In this case the farmer would pay a rent of 20 per cent, taken from his output (or "produce"), to the landlord.[1]

Rent does not emerge as a phenomenon in very early stages of a society's economic development, when fertile land is available in abundance. At this early stage of development, land would be similar to air and water, which is available in unlimited quantity and can therefore be appropriated without giving anything in exchange. It follows that rent can only be charged when land is limited in quantity.

Furthermore, land is not uniform in quality: some land is very fertile and can provide a large agricultural output, whereas other land is dry and not very useful. Farmers would be willing to pay more rent for a very fertile piece of land than for a very dry piece of land. It is also clear that in an early stage of development where land is freely available, the most fertile land would be taken into cultivation first. Now suppose that all the land of the highest quality has been taken into cultivation, and that there is a growth in population. Population growth implies that a society requires more food, and therefore more land must be cultivated to meet the demand. Since we have assumed that all the best-quality land has already been farmed, it follows that land of a lower quality must now be taken into cultivation. There would be competition between the farmers for the land of the highest quality, and the landlord will be able to charge a fee to the highest bidder for use of this highest-quality land. This fee will become the rent for the landlord, and would only be paid for the land of the highest quality. The land of the second-highest quality would not generate rent, because it is still freely available. If the population increases further, then at some point all the land of the second-highest quality would be cultivated, the result being that land of a lower quality would have to be farmed, in order to further increase food production. From then on, because of the competition between the farmers, the land of the second-highest quality would generate rent, and the rent for

---

1. The payment of rent is only for the "indestructible" powers of the soil, which excludes payments for the use of things such as buildings, fences or manure used to improve the quality of land. These latter payments are not part of the rent: they are profits for the landlords for the use of their capital. Farmers typically pay just one sum to the landlord, so it is not always clear which part of the payment is rent proper and which part is a reward for the use of capital. We will ignore this difficulty in our further discussion.

the land of the highest quality would increase. No rent would be paid for the land of the third-highest quality, as it would still be freely available (Ricardo 1817: 45–8). Given that this rent depends on extensive cultivation – or the amount of land that is currently being used – it can be called *extensive rent*. The *extensive margin of cultivation* is the least fertile land that is being used, and this land does not generate any rent (since it is still freely available).

From this example, we can conclude that rent emerges when the population grows and more food is required. Since the demand for food goes up, the price of food rises, and it is profitable for the farmer to produce more food to sell on the market. So far we have assumed that the farmer (assisted by her family) exerts her own labour on the land, but large farms typically employ labourers, which are hired by the farmer in exchange for wages. These wages must be paid by the farmer in advance of her selling her produce, as it takes time for the crops to grow, be harvested and finally be brought to market and sold. The farmer must therefore have a stock of *capital*, which she can use to pay the labourers before the fruits of their work are sold. Furthermore, the labourers need tools – such as spades – and seed in order to generate output for the farmer. The spades and seed must also be advanced by the farmer, and come out of her capital stock. When more land is taken into cultivation, more capital has to be applied: more labourers are hired, more wages are advanced, and the labourers will require additional spades and seed to do their jobs.

But there is also another possibility: rather than take more land into cultivation with the additional labourers (and therefore additional capital), the farmer could also employ the additional labourers on land that has already been cultivated. Instead of putting additional labourers (assisted by spades and seed) on land of the third and lowest quality (which is still freely available), the farmer could put the additional labourers on the land of the highest and/or second-highest quality (which has already been fully cultivated). Here, Ricardo assumes that doubling the amount of capital used on land with a given degree of fertility will increase the output generated by the land, but it will not double the output. In other words, there are *diminishing returns* to capital in agriculture: more capital will increase output, but at a decreasing rate.

Given that this capital will consist of advancing wages to the labourers and providing them with adequate tools and seed, we can also refer to doses of *capital-and-labour* that are applied to the land. Some doses of capital-and-labour will yield a high output (when deployed in favourable circumstances), others will yield a lower output (in less favourable circumstances). Every unit of any output will, however, be sold at the same price, no matter the conditions under which it was grown. Nobody would be willing to pay more for a potato because of the circumstances under which it was produced (assuming, of course, that all potatoes are identical). Since a unit of capital-and-labour applied in favourable circumstances would yield greater output, the landlord would be able to charge a higher rent than if that unit of capital-and-labour was applied in worse circumstances and yielded lower output: "rent is always the difference between the produce obtained by the employment of two equal quantities of capital and labour" (Ricardo 1817: 48). Given that this rent depends on intensive cultivation – the amount of capital-and-labour that is currently being used on land of a given quality – it can be called *intensive rent*. The *intensive margin of cultivation* is the unit of capital-and-labour that is used in the least favourable conditions, and this unit does not generate any rent.

Ricardo uses numerical examples to illustrate this theory, and this discussion can be clarified by using a table and a graph (Blaug 1962: 79–81). In this example, there are areas of land of five different qualities, A–E, with A being the highest quality and E the lowest, and the price of a bushel of corn is $1. Different amounts (or doses) of capital-and-labour can be applied to these different areas of land. If one dose of capital-and-labour costs $140, we can see in the table that the first dose of capital-and-labour applied to land A yields $180 (180 bushels of corn multiplied by the price of $1), giving a profit of $40 (the yield less the costs of capital-and-labour).

Capital and Labour	Total Product from Land					Marginal Product from Land				
	A	B	C	D	E	A	B	C	D	E
0	0	0	0	0	0					
						180	170	160	150	140
1	180	170	160	150	140					
						170	160	150	140	
2	350	330	310	290						
						160	150	140		
3	510	480	450							
						150	140			
4	660	620								
						140				
5	800									

Table 2.1 Total and marginal product on five grades of land of equal acreage.
Source: Blaug (1962: 78).

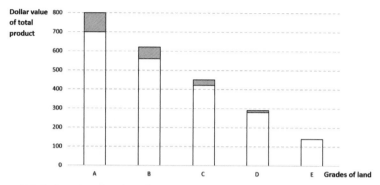

Figure 2.1 Dollar value of total product.
Source: Blaug (1962: 79).

A second dose of capital-and-labour applied to A would also be profitable, as the value of the output would then be $350 (taking into account the diminishing returns), which implies that the second dose adds an additional value of $170, giving a profit of $30 on the second dose. It would then be profitable to use five doses of capital-and-labour on land A, as the fifth dose would still increase the value of the output by $140, which is equal to the cost.

Working through the example, it would be profitable to apply four doses of capital-and-labour to land B, three to land C, two to land D and, finally, only one dose to land E. Since everybody would be willing to work on the best land and in the most favourable conditions, there would be competition between the farmers. Since the agricultural output is sold at a uniform price – every bushel of corn is sold at $1, irrespective of whether it was generated in the best or worst circumstances – the amount above $140 gained by any dose of capital-and-labour is the rent charged by the landowner. Since the last dose of capital-and-labour used on every land quality will generate only $140, there is no rent generated from the application of these doses. This implies that no rent at all will be generated on land E. On land D, two doses of capital-and-labour will be used for a total output worth $290, generating a rent of $10 from the first dose and none from the second. Land A generates $800, and therefore a rent of $100 ($800 – (5 × $140)) is paid, as five doses of capital-and-labour will have to be used. The last dose does not contribute to the rent; the fourth dose contributes $10; the third contributes $20; the second contributes $30; and the first dose, which is employed in the most

35

favourable circumstances, contributes $40 to the rent. The total amount of rent generated by every kind of land is represented by the shaded areas in the graph.

In summary, if the population increases and more food is required, the increasing demand for food implies that food prices rise. This makes it profitable for farmers to use more doses of capital-and-labour, either by taking land of a lower quality into cultivation or by adding more doses of capital-and-labour to the land that they are already cultivating. This implies that the rent paid for all previously used doses will increase, as only the doses deployed in the worst circumstances will not yield any rent. The implication here is that higher food prices translate into higher rent, and not the other way around (that higher rent creates higher food prices). In the previous chapter we saw that, according to Ricardo, the relative value of a unit of corn (and therefore its price) is determined by the amount of labour required for its production. We can now add that it is the amount of labour required for its production *in the least favourable circumstances*. A unit of corn produced in more favourable circumstances will be sold at the same price as a unit produced in less favourable circumstances, but it will generate a higher rent. In Ricardo's words:

> The value of corn is regulated by the quantity of labour bestowed on its production on that quality of land, or with that portion of capital, which pays no rent. Corn is not high because a rent is paid, but a rent is paid because corn is high.   (Ricardo 1817: 50)

In other words, rent is price determined and not price determining. Rent goes up when the food price increases, not the other way around. Rent is not a part of price, since all units of corn will be sold at the same price, irrespective of the conditions under which these units were produced. Corn produced in better circumstances will generate rent, but it will still be sold at the same price as corn produced in the worst circumstances. Therefore, rent is not part of the price of corn.

Following this logic, given that rent will go up when the food price increases and that the food price will increase when the population grows, a progressive nation with a growing population can expect to see increasing rents. These increasing rents lower the profits for the farmers. Eventually, the profit rate may fall to zero, and the economy ends up in a "stationary state", or a situation of zero economic growth. Since nobody will find it profitable to invest at a zero profit rate, economic progress would be checked in the "stationary state".[2]

The tendency of increasing rents is therefore a major problem that has preoccupied classical political economists. It may be explained as follows. Output is distributed into three main components: wages of labour, profits of capital, and rent of land. As we saw in the previous chapter, wages are fixed at subsistence level. Therefore, for any given output, higher rents must imply lower profits. When the farmers gain zero profits, their capital stock will not grow, and they will not be able to invest more (i.e. hire more labourers and buy more spades and seed). The economy stands still. This tendency may be countered by free trade in basic necessities, as this reduces the price of the goods consumed by the labourers, and therefore lowers the subsistence wages to be paid by the farmers.[3] Unsurprisingly, Ricardo was a strong advocate for free trade.[4] The problem of a prospective "stationary state" is ultimately caused by diminishing returns in agriculture. In the next section, we will explain that diminishing returns are not only evident in agriculture, but also in other sectors of the economy, such as manufacturing.

---

2. While this "stationary state" had never been observed, it was still a major issue for the classical economists. Note, however, that Mill (1848: 746–51) was not so negative about a possible stationary state, as moral and cultural progress would still remain possible.
3. Note that this only works for goods that are consumed by the labourers. If the cost of luxury goods decreases because of technological progress or cheaper imports, then the price of these luxury goods will go down. Consumers of luxury goods will be able to purchase more units of the luxury good for the same sum of money, but the profit rate will not be affected. Profits can only increase when wages go down, and given that wages are at subsistence level, wages can only go down when the prices of wage goods decrease.
4. To discuss the benefits of free trade, Ricardo (1817: 95–8) formulates his famous theory of comparative advantage. Even if, in absolute terms, England was more competitive in the production of both cloth and wine, it would still be beneficial to engage in international trade if England was relatively more competitive in the production of cloth (as compared to wine) and Portugal in the production of wine (as compared to cloth). England would reach a higher level of consumption if it specialized in the production of cloth and then exchanged the cloth for wine produced in Portugal; Portugal would also reach a higher level of consumption if it specialized in the production of wine and then exchanged the wine for cloth produced in England. This effect would even occur if England, as in Ricardo's numerical example, was able to produce both cloth and wine at a lower cost compared to Portugal – the point is that England is relatively more efficient in the production of cloth than in the production of wine (and the opposite is the case for Portugal).

Longfield's lectures

The Irish economist Samuel Mountifort Longfield (1802–84) elaborates on the theory of rent in his *Lectures on Political Economy Delivered in Trinity and Michaelmas Terms* (the lectures were delivered in 1833 and published in 1834). Rent is settled by contract and is dependent on the principles of supply and demand: the available fertile land provided by the landlords (supply) for which the farmers will compete (demand). Land that is more fertile, or nearer to a suitable market, will then yield a higher rent than land that is less fertile, or located somewhere less favourable. He repeats the argument that rent is price determined and that it does not form a part of the price of the agricultural produce. He also states that rent does not form a part of the cost of production, as rent does not depend on the amount of output that is generated by the farmer. Modern economists would call the rent a *fixed cost*: no matter how many units of corn the farmer decides to produce, the amount of rent to be paid to the landlord will remain the same. The cost of production of a bushel of corn depends on the amount of labour, spades and seed (paid in advance from the farmer's capital stock) required for its production – modern economists would term these *variable costs*.

We saw above that there are diminishing returns to capital in agriculture, which implies that the variable costs of production increase when more capital is being used. Ever more units of labour, spades and seed will be required to produce additional bushels of corn. Therefore, the price of corn will have to increase, as it will become ever more costly to produce additional corn. Longfield indicates, however, that the variable cost of production has no immediate effect on the price or the value of a good – but it does affect it indirectly. A higher cost of production would limit supply, since farmers will not find it profitable to produce corn when they cannot cover their costs of production. This limitation in supply will, in turn, increase the price of corn. Rent, on the other hand, cannot diminish the supply: as a fixed cost, a reduction in supply would not generate more revenue in order to pay the rent. In Longfield's words, the manager of the farm

> will cultivate his farm in such a manner, as according to the average price of agricultural produce, will leave the greatest surplus after paying all the expenses of cultivation with the usual profits of stock. The average amount of what this surplus is, on the supposition that

the cultivation is conducted with average skill, is what the landlord may reasonably demand for rent.   (Longfield 1934: 120–1)

The amount of rent is therefore determined by the average amount of surplus (the price of output minus variable costs) that the farmer with average skill can be expected to produce. If the landlord were to charge less to a certain farmer, then the latter would be outbid by other farmers; if the landlord charges more, then no farmer would find it profitable to cultivate the land in the first place.

Given that rent is a fixed charge, it does not enter into the cost of production, which is determined by the manner in which the farmer cultivates the land, i.e. by applying capital and labour. Longfield then formulates the principle of diminishing returns:

In general, by increasing the labour and expense of cultivating a farm, its gross produce may be increased, but not in the same proportion; and by diminishing the labour and expense of cultivation, the gross produce will be diminished, but not in the same proportion.   (Longfield 1934: 124)

These diminishing returns mean that when population increases and the demand for food rises, the price of food must rise in order to make it profitable for a farmer to use more units of capital and labour in agricultural production (either by using existing land more intensively, or by taking land of a lower quality into cultivation): "What is really necessary and sufficient is, that the price of the produce raised *by the last outlay or expense* shall be sufficient to repay that expense, with common profits" (Longfield 1834: 128; my emphasis). While Longfield does not use the word "margin", he expresses the principle of marginalism: the farmer will compare the cost of an additional dose of capital-and-labour with the price he can get for the additional output, in order to decide whether to use this additional dose or not. Using an additional dose of capital-and-labour will extend the extensive margin of cultivation when land of a lower quality is being cultivated, or extend the intensive margin of cultivation when more doses of capital-and-labour are used on land that had already been taken into cultivation. Given that there are diminishing returns, the variable cost of production will rise. The cost of production (or the natural price) of a good will then be equal to the cost of producing the good in the worst circumstances (the margin of cultivation, where no rent is paid). The theory of rent can be summarized in two propositions:

> First, that the rent of land depends upon its fertility and situation, and upon the price of agricultural produce. Secondly, that the cost of production, or natural price of agricultural produce, depends upon and is regulated by the expense of producing that portion which is raised with the greatest amount of labour [i.e. which is produced in the least favourable circumstances].
>
> (Longfield 1834: 136)

So far Longfield has mentioned the "usual profits" or "common profits" of the farmer, but it remains unclear at this point how these "common profits" are determined, or, in other words, what the rate of profits should be. As we saw before, the profits are the payment made by the labourer for the use of the farmer's capital stock. Since the farmer advances wages to the labourer, he needs to receive a "discount" from the labourer for being paid promptly: "The rate of profits depends upon the proportion which exists between the advance made by the capitalist, and the return which he receives, and the length of time for which that advance is made" (Longfield 1834: 170).

While Longfield's arguments are generally in line with other writers of classical political economy, he disagrees with the idea that the decreasing fertility of the land (and therefore diminishing returns in agriculture, which imply increasing rent) is the cause of a falling profit rate. First of all, in prosperous times wages might rise above the subsistence level, and therefore part of the increased rent can be borne by the labourer. Second, and more importantly, Longfield argues that the rate of profit might also fall because more capital is being used (in the absence of technological progress and population growth) on the purchase of machinery. (Note that the rate of profit is established for the economy as a whole, which includes both agriculture and manufacturing,[5] and that machines are mainly used in manufacturing.)

---

5. Note that the invisible hand mechanism (see previous chapter) will make sure that the profit rates in agriculture and manufacturing are equalized. If the profit rate in agriculture fell below the profit rate in manufacturing, then capital would be withdrawn

Machines for manufacturing are similar to land for agriculture, in that they operate with various degrees of efficiency, just as land manifests itself in various degrees of fertility. Labourers (or manufacturers who employ labourers) will compete to purchase or rent the machine that makes their labour most productive, just as farmers will compete to rent the land that provides the most favourable circumstances. This competition between labourers (or between manufacturers who employ labourers) will increase the price or the rent for the machine, just as the competition between farmers will increase the rent for the land. A key difference between machines and land, however, is that machines can be produced, whereas land is a gift of nature and only exists in limited supply. A higher price for a certain machine will therefore encourage its manufacturers to make that machine. When more machines of a certain kind become available, the makers of these machines will have to lower their price in order to increase their sales.

In other words, we have here an instance of the "invisible hand mechanism", which was discussed in the previous chapter: competition between labourers (or between manufacturers who employ labourers) will change the prices for different kinds of machines (with various degrees of efficiency), and competition between the makers of these machines will equalize the level of profit for the production of these machines: "This level [of profit] must be determined by the less efficient machine, since the sum paid for its use can never exceed the value of the assistance it gives to the labourer" (Longfield 1834: 187–8). This can be explained by investigating the maximum amount that a labourer would be willing to pay for any machine.

In the first instance, the maximum amount that the labourer would be willing to pay is the value of the work that would be saved. Suppose that the machine with the highest degree of efficiency could double the output of a labourer: she produces 100 units of output (per hour) without the machine, but 200 units with the machine. Using the machine would therefore generate an additional output of 100 units. The labourer would

---

from agriculture and transferred to manufacturing. Supply of goods would decrease in agriculture, the price of agricultural goods would increase, and the profit rate in agriculture would rise again. The opposite would happen in manufacturing: supply will increase, the price will decrease and so will the profit rate. Eventually, the profit rates in agriculture and manufacturing will be equalized.

then not be willing to pay more than 100 units of her output for using the machine, since at a higher price she would do better without the machine.

In the second instance, the maximum amount that the labourer would be willing to pay for any machine would be determined by the price of the available, less efficient machines. Suppose that there are less efficient machines available on the market, that would less than double the output of the labourer: for instance, the machine would enable a labourer to generate 150 units of output, compared with 100 units of output without the machine. If that machine costs 25 units of output, then the labourer would have a net surplus of 150 – 100 – 25 = 25 units from using this less efficient machine compared with using no machine at all. The supplier of the most efficient machine would then no longer be able to charge up to 100 units of output, but only 100 – 25 = 75 units, since at a higher price the labourer would still do better with the less efficient machine:

> Thus the sum which can be paid for the use of any machine has its greatest limit determined by its efficiency in assisting the operations of the labourer, while its lesser limit is determined by the efficiency of that capital which without imprudence is employed in the least efficient manner. (Longfield 1834: 188)

In other words, the maximum price for a machine is limited not only by the additional production of the labourer using the machine, but also by the net surplus (additional output minus price) of the least efficient available machine (which is the machine at the margin). The level of profit is therefore determined "by the profits of that capital which is naturally the least efficiently employed" (Longfield 1834: 188). In modern terms we would speak of *opportunity costs*: the amount of profit that your capital could generate elsewhere. Any new unit of capital entering the market would encounter the conditions at the margin, with the lowest profit rate (in the absence of technological progress).

We could also say that there are diminishing returns to capital: newly added units of capital will generate less profit than units that were added previously. If the owner of capital were to own a spade, then she would naturally hire the most efficient labourer and give her the spade to assist her labour. Once capital has been accumulated and more spades can be bought, the capitalist will necessarily have to hire less efficient labourers, given that she has already employed the most efficient one.

The rate of profit of a spade will then be determined by the difference between the surplus generated by the least efficient labourer with and without the use of the spade. If the profits were higher, then the labourers would earn more by not using the spade (since they would not have to pay the owner of the spade); the demand for spades would go down, the price of spades would decrease and, finally, the profit rate for producing spades would go down. If profits were lower, then the competition between the labourers would make the least efficient labourers accept lower wages (which would increase profits again). When more spades become available in the economy (because of capital accumulation), they cannot be employed with equal effect, and therefore the rate of profit must decline.

Without using the word, Longfield applies the principle of the "margin" – which had already been applied to the theory of rent – to the theory of profits.[6] His exact calculation of the rate of profit is, however, rather complicated. First of all, Longfield emphasizes that the decrease in profits (and/or wages) caused by increasing rent "proceed[s] by imperceptibly small differences, and not by sudden steps" (Longfield 1834: 185). Second, the varying length of time of the production processes makes "the calculation more complex" (Longfield 1934: 209–16). Modern economists have come to realize that the calculation becomes less complex if a form of mathematics is used that deals with these "imperceptibly small differences": namely, differential calculus (which describes the rate of change at a given point). But the economists of the early nineteenth century did not make use of calculus. Johann Heinrich von Thünen, whose work on the "isolated state" is discussed further below, is a notable exception. First, though, we need to say something more about the use of calculus in economics, since this is essential for an understanding of the further development of marginalism.

---

6. He does not apply the same principle to the determination of wages, as they depend entirely on the rate of profit (which is paid by the labourer for the use of the capital) and on the productiveness of the labour (a more productive labourer will receive a higher wage compared with a less productive labourer). The extension of marginalist theory to the determination of the rate of wages was discussed by Jevons (see chapter 4) and fully worked out by Clark (see chapter 7).

Calculus and economics

We have seen above that it was difficult for Longfield to determine the rate of profits, since several factors play a role: (a) the amount that was advanced by the farmer (which includes the wages); (b) the total amount of output and the price at which that output is sold; and (c) the length of time of the production process. In every economic model, there are many variables that interact with each other, and it is very difficult to disentangle this web using simple mathematics and numerical examples. Economists such as Ricardo and Longfield could not come to exact mathematical expressions about this matter (and basically decided to ignore these complex calculations).

A second and related matter concerns the "imperceptibly small differences" that were mentioned by Longfield: economic change can be a long process in which different variables (such as profits, wages, supply and demand) interact with each other incrementally. Thünen (1850: 410) states that differential calculus is required: if a function (such as the profit rate) is influenced by different variables (such as the wage rate and the length of time of production), then we can first regard wages as constant and maximize profits by changing the length of time, and then regard the length of time as constant and maximize profits by changing the wage rate. This process of maximization takes place in "imperceptibly" small steps, and differential calculus is the right mathematical tool to complete the mission.

Given that differential calculus plays an important role in understanding marginalism, it is worth considering how it works. Calculus is "differential" when it deals with differences: for instance, what happens to the rate of profits if the rate of wages changes? Given that several other factors (or variables) may impact the rate of profits, traditional mathematics can be helpful only to a certain extent. In differential calculus we focus solely on the relationship between profits and wages, keeping everything else (such as the length of time of the production process) constant. We can then vary the rate of wages, and see what impact this has on the rate of profits. Suppose that we use the symbol π to denote profits and the symbol w to denote wages, then we can examine how a change in wages (Δw, with the Greek character Δ indicating a change) will generate a change in profits ($\Delta \pi$), keeping everything else constant. Given that changes often take place in imperceptibly small steps, we want to know what happens to profits when wages change in imperceptibly small steps – modern mathematicians would speak instead about "infinitesimally" small steps; differential calculus can also be described as the mathematics of the infinite. We can illustrate this with the following graph.

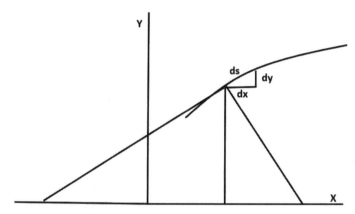

Figure 2.2 Differential calculus.
Source: Antognazza (2016: 23).

The relationship between the two variables x and y is given by the curved line, which expresses that y is a function of x – when x changes, then y will also change in a certain way. The amount of change is measured by the curvature. It tells us by how much y will change (denoted by dy) if there is a change in x (denoted by dx). Differential calculus means that we make the change of x infinitely small. The little "triangle" below the curve will then shrink to one point, and we can apply elementary geometry to determine the amount of curvature (which is the derivative).

This mathematical procedure can only work when the curve is continuous, which means that there are no "jumps" in the curve: it has to be a fluent line. This means that variables would have to be allowed to change in infinitesimally small steps. While it is obvious that in reality wages would not change in infinitesimally small steps (a change in wages should have the magnitude of at least a cent, or the smallest denomination of the currency being used), the application of calculus to economics requires that we regard our magnitudes as continuous functions, in which the variables can indeed change in small steps that approach zero. By letting Δw shrink to zero, we get dw, which is the continuous version of the change in wages Δw.[7] This allows us to see the change in profits $\Delta \pi$, which we also describe by its continuous version as $d\pi$. We can do this for all variables that influence the rate of profits, and find out how an infinitesimally small change in any of these variables will change profits.

In mathematical terms, this allows us to maximize a given function (the profits that we typically want to maximize) if it is a multivariate function, i.e. if it depends on multiple variables. The relative impact of wages on profits would first be seen as the ratio $\Delta \pi / \Delta w$, which is the change in profits, caused only by the change in wages (since everything else was assumed to remain constant), divided by the change in wages. By letting the change in wages shrink to (or approach) zero (which means by making it infinitesimally small), we get the calculus version of the impact of wages on profits, which is $d\pi/dw$. This latter expression is the first derivative of profits to wages, or the expression that tells us what would happen to profits if wages were to change by an infinitesimally small amount, leaving everything else constant.

This first derivative also tells us what the direction of the influence may be. In classical political economy there is a negative relationship between profits and wages (if wages go up, profits go down), so we would expect the first derivative $d\pi/dw$ to have a negative sign. If the relationship were positive, then the first derivative would have a positive sign. This also implies that if $d\pi/dw$ were equal to zero, then we would have a maximum or a minimum: an infinitesimally small change in wages would not change profits at all. To conclude: differential calculus allows us to maximize (or minimize) multivariate functions by investigating every variable separately, leaving everything else constant, and finding out what the effect is on the function of an infinitesimally small change in any of these variables.

---

7. The symbol Δ – Delta – is actually a Greek "D", and therefore both symbols are used to express "difference" or "change". It is customary to represent continuous change with "d" and discontinuous changes with "Δ", given that the relevant mathematics – Euclidean geometry – was developed in Greek antiquity. Differential calculus – the mathematics of the continuous – was only developed around 1700, by both Newton and Leibniz, and it has become customary to represent continuous changes with Latin characters.

Thünen's isolated state

The writings of Johann Heinrich von Thünen (1783–1850) are comparable to the works of classical authors such as Ricardo and Longfield, but his application of calculus makes him a forerunner of later marginalist authors such as Jevons (see chapter 4) and Walras (see chapter 5). Thünen was a landowner, and he used the data from his own farm to develop his theory about the "isolated state". This hypothetical state is isolated from the rest of the world because it is surrounded by territory that cannot be crossed. Modern economists would call this a "closed economy", as opposed to an "open economy", which is connected to the rest of the world through international trade.

In this isolated state (as in the rest of the world), wages are typically low, so the question arises of whether rents and profits are too high, leaving insufficient room for labourers to make a decent living. The owners of land (the landlords) and the owners of capital (the capitalists) claim an excessive part of the output, leaving only subsistence wages for the labourers, i.e. just enough to survive and to raise a family.

Thünen describes this as an important societal problem, for which economists cannot provide an answer. He states that this perceived injustice may fuel the revolutionary forces of socialists and communists, which may bring bloodshed and turmoil to the world (Thünen 1850: 435–8). In order to prevent such a violent revolution, Thünen examines what would happen if the inhabitants of the "isolated state" were to come to a rational and reasonable distribution of the state's economic product.[8] He notes that common labourers typically get married at around the age of 20, whereas civil servants and other more highly educated people marry later, once they are over 30. This implies that there will be relatively more common labourers with a low level of education, and that their wages will be low, given there is a high number of them. These labourers do not have the "drive" to provide a good education for their children, nor do they have the financial means to make a good education possible. If the state were to provide this education, then more children of labourers would want to become civil servants. As a

---

8. Thünen's approach can be understood as an application of German idealistic philosophy, particularly that of Georg Wilhelm Friedrich Hegel (1770–1831), which implies an attempt to simultaneously discuss the issue of distribution from theoretical (positive) and practical (normative) points of view.

consequence, there would be fewer common labourers and more civil servants. The wages of common labourers would then increase and the wages of civil servants would go down. Furthermore, a more educated population would have a positive impact on scientific development and therefore on the productivity of labour: a single unit of labour would now produce more output than before.

Thünen regards this story as "a dream", which he wrote down when he studied the works of earlier classical economists (including Ricardo), which according to Thünen did not provide a satisfactory treatment of the wage rate (Thünen 1850: 440–4). As we saw in the previous chapter, classical economists maintained that wages can only rise when profits go down (and vice versa), and the Malthusian theory of population explains why wages must necessarily be at subsistence level. Such conclusions arose because the classical economists used *inductive* reasoning: namely, they proceeded from the facts in order to establish a theory. For Thünen, the correct way to proceed is using *deductive* reasoning, i.e. starting from a theory in order to derive conclusions, per the natural sciences of the day (Thünen 1850: 458–62). As we will see, in deductive reasoning the application of calculus turns out to be very instrumental.

In diagram form, the isolated state is a collection of concentric circles: the city centre is the heart of economic activity, where all the trading takes place. All forms of production are located optimally around this city centre, with the distance to the centre determined by the durability of the good and the transportation costs. Thünen turns his attention to the outer border of the isolated state, where we find the least productive circumstances. As we have seen, this is the margin of a society, where the rent of land is zero. Therefore, all output generated at this outer border will be divided between profits and wages only.

Thünen does not assume from the outset that wages are at subsistence level. However, any labourer would have to earn *at least* the subsistence wage, just enough to survive and to reproduce the family, which he denotes by the symbol a. The part of the wage that is not strictly necessary for subsistence can be designated by y, so that the wage of the labourer, denoted by the symbol A, would be equal to the sum of a and y, and therefore $A = a + y$ (Thünen 1850: 476–7).

That surplus y could be used for consumption, but it could also be accumulated and turned into capital. For instance, suppose that a labourer requires 100 units of food per year for survival (his subsistence wage a) but that he can produce 110 units of food per year (his total wage A). He could then consume an additional 10 units of food per year (a luxury purchase y, since those 10 units are not strictly required for survival), but he could also save the 10 units for later consumption (assuming that the food would not spoil). If he saves an extra 10 units year-on-year, then after 10 years he would have a pile of 100 units, which would allow him to take a break from cultivation and spend his time developing useful tools (which are capital goods), such as spades.

Suppose that a spade would allow him to produce 150 units of food per year (as opposed to 110 units without the spade). He could then decide to provide other labourers with his spades and get paid for the use of his equipment. Given that the other labourer would be able to produce 150 units of food (with a spade) rather than 110 (without a spade), the first labourer would be able to charge up to 40 units for the use of the spade. Given that the production of spades turns out to be very profitable, after a while more labourers may decide to produce spades. This suggests that there will be competition between producers of spades, and therefore the price to be paid for the use of a spade will have to go down. Hence, when a new technology is introduced (i.e. when the first spade is made), substantial profits can be generated initially, but as the idea catches on and more people turn to manufacturing spades, the profits from this product will decrease.

Here, Thünen has observed the similarity between the use of land and capital goods (spades) that was already identified by Longfield: units added at an earlier stage generate more revenue than units that are added at a later stage (Thünen 1850: 484–94). In a more developed stage of a society, two classes of labourers will emerge: those who produce spades and those who borrow the spades from the first class in order to produce food. The wage of the second class is then equal to the output of their labour minus the amount charged for the capital (namely, the *interest* paid on the loan of the spades: typically a fixed amount that is paid regularly as a percentage of the value of the spades). Since one spade is equal to another spade, the accumulation of capital (the increase in the number of spades) must imply that the interest must go down: a larger supply of spades implies a lower price for spades, and therefore a lower interest payment from the second to the first class of labourers. An important "marginalist" conclusion emerges, again similar to that stated by Longfield: "The interest, granted by the borrowed capital as a whole, is determined by the use of the lastly invested unit of capital" (Thünen 1850: 498).[9]

While the theories of Thünen and Longfield are similar so far, Thünen also applies differential calculus to determine the wage rate. Essentially, there are two factors that have an impact on wage rates, which the labourers want to maximize. On the one hand, it is clear that wages will increase if the interest – paid for the use of the capital – decreases. So it seems that wages would be maximized if the payment for the capital is reduced to zero. On the other hand, more capital (tools such as spades) would increase the productivity of labour, and therefore the output per unit of labour (denoted by Thünen as p) would be raised. At zero interest, no capital would be produced, as nobody would find it worthwhile to save and to devote time to producing spades, and therefore the output per unit of labour (p) would go down. Given that we have here a multivariate function (the wage rate), we need to apply differential calculus to find out at which point the wages for the labourer are maximized. There should be enough capital (and therefore interest) to increase labour productivity, but interest payments should also not be too high, in order to leave enough room for the labourer's wages.

It would go beyond the scope of this book to follow Thünen's argument in detail, but he concludes that the wage of the labourer ($A = a + y$) should be, from both a theoretical and a practical (moral) point of view, equal to $\sqrt{ap}$, or the square root of the product of a (the necessary subsistence) and p (the output per unit of labour, which increases when more capital (tools such as spades) are being used).[10]

Thünen's analysis is somewhat fragmented and obscure, but he should be credited for having applied differential calculus to the problems of economics. Like Longfield, Thünen arrives at a "marginalist" explanation for the rate of profits: it is determined by the last unit of capital, which is used in the least productive circumstances. The marginalist analysis is, however, still incomplete: no general model of productive factors (land, capital and labour) emerges, and the reasoning is restricted to the supply side of the economy. We have seen that there are diminishing returns in both agriculture and manufacturing, which implies that additional (or "marginal") units

---

9. "Die Rente, die das Kapital im ganzen beim Ausleihen gewährt, wird bestimmt durch die Nutzung des zuletzt angelegten Kapitalteilchens"(my translation).
10. See Blaug (1985) for a more elaborate description and critical analysis of the work of von Thünen.

can only be realized at increasing cost, and that output therefore increases at a decreasing rate. A similar phenomenon occurs on the demand side of the economy: consumer satisfaction increases when more units are consumed, but also at a decreasing rate. This application of marginalism to the demand side requires the development of utility theory, which we will examine in the next chapter.

3

Demand-side marginalism: Gossen as a forerunner of marginalism

Thünen has much in common with Gossen: both authors published in German, and both authors applied differential calculus to economic analysis. Moreover, both authors were ignored by their contemporaries, and did not live to see the positive comments made about their innovative works by later marginalists such as Jevons (see chapter 4) or Marshall (see chapter 7).

But whereas Thünen investigated the supply side of the economy, Gossen turned his attention to demand. We will start by investigating his *Development of the Laws of Human Intercourse and the Consequent Rules of Human Action,* which was completed in 1853 and published in 1854. In this work, Gossen investigates how consumers make choices – or rather, how they *should* make choices – by comparing the pleasure that is provided through the consumption of different goods. In order to acquire these goods, individuals must provide labour to earn income with which to buy them, and that labour is usually painful and must therefore also be taken into account. Whereas Gossen's "doctrine of enjoyment" relies on pleasure (and its opposite: pain), later marginalists would use the term "utility" (and "disutility") to describe the potential that an object has to provide pleasure (or pain) for an individual consumer.

The second part of this chapter therefore analyses this important concept. The term "utility" was already widely used by French economists (*"utilité"*), but it lacked a proper definition until it was provided by Jules Dupuit (1804–66), who also elaborated on how "utility" should be properly measured.

Gossen's laws of human enjoyment

The background to Gossen's analysis is a positivistic and religious world view.[1] According to Gossen, an individual being should organize his/her life in such a way that the total sum of all enjoyment over his/her lifetime is maximized. In other words, individuals should try to maximize their pleasures over the total duration of their lifetime.

This does not imply that individuals should simply consume as much as possible, since the achievement of some pleasure (*"Genuss"*) in the present may be followed by some pain (*"Entbehrung"*) in the future. For instance, the enjoyment of excessive amounts of food and drink may be enjoyable tonight but will probably generate pain tomorrow morning. Most people will probably agree that pleasure should be maximized, but they will not necessarily agree about the precise quantity of all possible enjoyment. Nevertheless, it sounds almost straightforward that everybody should try to maximize the amount of pleasure they enjoy during their lifetime.

Even an ascetic person, who tries to avoid consumption as much as possible, acts according to this principle: the enjoyments on earth are not sufficient for the ascetic person, so he tries to maximize, through his ascetic behaviour, the enjoyments that he will achieve in the afterlife, in which he firmly believes. The general rule for any individual is, therefore, that his or her behaviour should be set up in such a way as to maximize the total sum of his or her enjoyment (Gossen 1854: 1–4).

Gossen argues that all pleasures have two common characteristics. First of all, the size of a certain pleasure decreases continuously as the enjoyment of the pleasure continues, until eventually saturation takes place. For instance, the first mouthful of a meal always tastes better than the second, which in turn tastes better than the third. Second, if the enjoyment of a certain pleasure is repeated at a later point in time, then the magnitude of this pleasure will also be lower compared with the

---

1. Gossen's argument is that the Creator (*"der Schöpfer"*) must have deliberately created the force (*"die Kraft"*) in humanity that urges us to strive for a maximum of enjoyments. This desire should not be condemned as such, but it should be understood properly. The commandment of the Creator is: "Human! Study the laws of my creation, and act according to these laws!" (*"Mensch! Erforsche die Gesetze meiner Schöpfung, und diesen Gesetzen gemäss handle!"* (Gossen 1854: 4), my translation).

original enjoyment of the pleasure. For instance, if you consume the same food every day, then the pleasure derived from consuming this food will decrease over time.

These two characteristics do not apply solely to the consumption of material goods, as the following example illustrates. A work of art, such as a painting, provides enjoyment to its owner. The enjoyment is experienced when the owner looks at the work, but this enjoyment will decrease over time, and at some point saturation will occur and the owner will cease to look at the artwork. The enjoyment will be greatest the first time the art is viewed, it will decrease the second time, then again the third time, and so on. The owner of the artwork will leave ever-longer periods of time in between two observations of the work, and the duration of the enjoyment will decrease with every additional observation. Training ("*Übung*") of the senses – such as sight, hearing, taste – or of the mind may increase the pleasure derived from these senses in general, but it cannot counteract the tendency for the level of pleasure derived from the repetitive enjoyment of one and the same object to diminish (Gossen 1854: 4–7).

In order to clarify this important tendency, Gossen proceeds with a geometrical representation. He recognizes that it is not possible to directly measure enjoyment, but he does not exclude the possibility that such a measurement could be made in the future. Nevertheless, a geometrical representation adds to understanding, given that not only the mind but also the eye can now be used to improve comprehension. Furthermore, if the geometrical representation is correct, then mathematics can be used for further analysis.

Figure 3.1 represents the time by the line a–b (the *x*-axis), during which a certain enjoyment lasts (starting at point a, ending at point b). The first and initial enjoyment, during the time period a–d, is the greatest: it is represented by the area a–d–e–c. During the second period of time, represented by d–f, there is still a large amount of enjoyment, represented by the area d–f–g–e, but it is smaller than the first area. During the third period of time, represented by f–h, there will be an even smaller area of enjoyment. And so it continues. The diagram therefore represents Gossen's important observation that enjoyment decreases over time. This decrease may be represented in different ways, as illustrated by Figures 3.2–3.4.

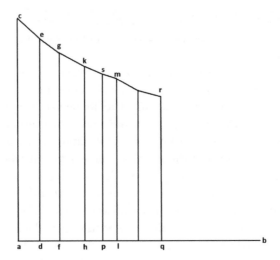

Figure 3.1 Decrease of enjoyment over time.
Source: Gossen (1854: 8).

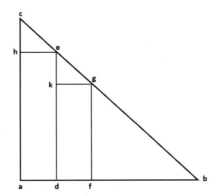

Figure 3.2 Decrease of enjoyment over time: straight line.
Source: Gossen (1854: 9).

These three diagrams all have in common that saturation occurs at point b, which means that a continued consumption of the good beyond this point will no longer increase the pleasure of the consumer: saturation occurs. A curve can be drawn from point c on top – the initial and highest amount of pleasure – towards point b at the bottom, where continued consumption will no longer add to the pleasure as saturation has occurred.

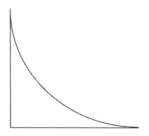

Figure 3.3 Decrease of enjoyment over time: curved line (convex).
Source: Gossen (1854: 9).

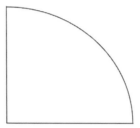

Figure 3.4 Decrease of enjoyment over time: curved line (concave).
Source: Gossen (1854: 9).

Given that we have no precise information about the curve, the most straightforward assumptions should be based on Figure 3.2, in which the curve c–b is a straight line. The straight line implies that the decrease in pleasure is linear and continuous: for equal amounts of time, the decline in pleasure will be identical. The triangle a–b–c will then correspond to the total amount of pleasure derived from the consumption of the good during the time a–b. Continued consumption of one and the same good will make this triangle smaller, as can be seen in Figure 3.5: the initial enjoyment will become smaller (c' is smaller than c) and saturation will occur earlier (b' is smaller than b).

An extreme case would be continued consumption of one and the same good to the extent that the triangle a–b–c shrunk to the point a only. This would happen if we continued consumption even after saturation had set in, and from then on continued consumption forever. An example is daylight, which we do not generally experience as pleasurable unless we have been deprived of it for a certain amount of time. This experience also depends on the point of view of the consumer: the landscape of the countryside, which may attract a large number of tourists, does not provide enjoyment for the farmer who works in the area every day (Gossen 1854: 7–11).

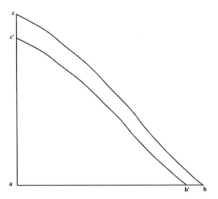

Figure 3.5 Decrease of enjoyment over time: continued consumption.

Source: Gossen (1854: 9).

Gossen derives three propositions from these observations. The first one summarizes what was said above:

> For each individual enjoyment, there are ways and means to enjoy it, which depend primarily on the frequency of the repetition of that enjoyment, by which the accumulation of enjoyment reaches its height. When this maximum has been attained, then this sum of enjoyment is diminished by a more frequent as well as by a less frequent repetition. (Gossen 1854: 11; my translation)[2]

In other words, an individual can maximize their amount of enjoyment by carefully considering, for every form of enjoyment, how often they repeat it. But once saturation has set in, repeating this form of enjoyment will no longer increase the total amount of enjoyment, but will rather decrease it. This implies that other forms of enjoyment, for which saturation has not been reached yet, should come into the frame. Time needs to pass before the initial form of enjoyment becomes pleasurable again. A bad example of this,

---

2. Note that this formulation is not the same as what is currently known as 'Gossen's first law', which simply states that marginal utility decreases when consumption increases. For more about the interpretation of Gossen's laws, see Jolink and van Daal (1998).

provided by Gossen, is Louis XV, the king of France: his continued exposure to all imaginable enjoyments reduced his pleasures to such an extent that only boredom ("*Langeweile*") remained.

Given that we need to distribute our time over different forms of possible enjoyment, in order to avoid saturation and achieve the highest amount of pleasure, this leads us to Gossen's second proposition:

> A person, who is free to choose between different enjoyments, but whose time is not sufficient to fully realize them all, must realize all of them partially, however different the absolute magnitudes of the individual enjoyments might be, in order to maximize the sum of his enjoyment, before he even fully realizes the greatest enjoyment, and in such a way *that the magnitude of each enjoyment in that moment, in which the enjoyment ends, remains the same for all.*
>
> (Gossen 1854: 12; original emphasis; my translation)

In other words, when an individual can choose between different forms of enjoyment, then he or she should make sure that the last moments of time spent on every form of enjoyment provide the same amount of pleasure. This proposition can be illustrated with the triangular diagrams in Figure 3.6.

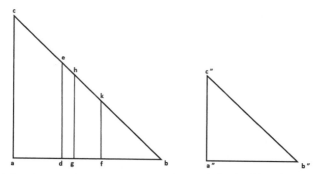

Figure 3.6 Distribution of time over two different forms of enjoyment.
Source: Gossen (1854: 13).

Suppose that an individual can choose between two forms of enjoyment (represented, respectively, by the large triangle on the left and the smaller triangle on the right). Given that the initial amount of pleasure for the first enjoyment is larger than for the second (the length a–c in the left diagram versus the length a"–c" in the right diagram), the first enjoyment will initially provide more pleasure than the second.

Unfortunately, continued enjoyment will decrease the amount of additional pleasure: we move on the line c–b towards point b, at which saturation occurs. As soon as we spend an amount of time a–d on the first enjoyment, the additional pleasure that we could derive from this continued enjoyment will become smaller than the initial pleasure that we would derive from the second enjoyment: for instance, the length a"–c" (the initial pleasure of the second enjoyment) is larger than the length g–h or the length f–k. Therefore, we should switch from the first enjoyment to the second enjoyment as soon as an amount of time a–d has been spent on the first enjoyment.

Continuing with the second enjoyment will, however, also decrease the amount of additional pleasure derived from the second enjoyment, which at some point would make it beneficial to switch back to the first enjoyment. It follows, therefore, that we maximize our total amount of pleasure by distributing our time over the two forms of enjoyment in such a way that the amount of pleasure gained by the last moments of time spent on the first and second forms of enjoyment would be equal. This reasoning can be extended to three or four or more different forms of enjoyment (Gossen 1854: 12–13).

Once we have distributed our time optimally over all possible forms of enjoyment, by making sure that the last second that we spent on each of the forms gives us an equal amount of pleasure, we could increase our total amount of pleasure further by discovering new forms of enjoyment, or by training or changing the environment in which the form of enjoyment occurs. The third proposition states:

> The possibility of increasing the sum of the enjoyment during his lifetime, under the given circumstances, is available to an individual every time a new enjoyment is discovered, be it ever so small, or by increasing a known enjoyment through education or by influencing the outside world. (Gossen 1854: 21; my translation)

For example, the boredom of Louis XV could have been avoided if he had filled his time with learning about ever more new forms of enjoyment or with improving his skills. It follows that mankind must use the arts and the sciences to discover all possible forms of enjoyment, as well as the means to improve these enjoyments (by personal training or by altering the environment) (Gossen 1854: 22–3).

Gossen on value

This brings Gossen to the question of "value", which he approaches from a completely different perspective to the "classical" economists. Since humans try to maximize pleasure, it follows that the "value" of the outside world depends on the amount of pleasure that humans can derive from it.

The objects of the outside world can be classified into three groups. The objects of the first group can be consumed directly and provide immediate enjoyment – Gossen calls these the "means of enjoyment". This includes objects that are provided by nature, such as an apple, but also objects created by people, such as a meal prepared by a cook or a chair made by a carpenter. Since the apple and the meal provide enjoyment only once, their value is determined by the amount of pleasure generated by their consumption. Since the chair can be used several times, the value of the chair is equal to the sum of all enjoyments of its use, until it is completely worn out. Other objects, such as a house or a painting, typically last longer than a human life, so the value of such an object for a specific individual is equal to the sum of all the enjoyments that can be derived from it during his lifetime.

A second group of objects, which Gossen simply calls "objects of the second class", are things that do not provide direct enjoyment but are nonetheless necessary in order to generate certain kinds of enjoyment. For instance, we use a fireplace in order to receive warmth (which we enjoy), but we also need fire and firewood. If we want to enjoy music, we need not only a flute but also a musician to play it. The enjoyment is only possible when all these different objects are united, but it is not possible to pin down the exact contribution of each of them to the enjoyment. We can value the enjoyment of the warmth, but we cannot clearly indicate how much value was provided by the fireplace, the fire or the firewood. Both the musician and the flute contribute to the enjoyment, but it is unclear how much value can be attributed to each of them; it is only clear that we need both in order to make enjoyment possible.

Finally, "objects of the third class" can never become "means of enjoyment" (the first class) or parts of these "means of enjoyment" (the second class), but are instead used to produce objects of the first or second class.

This class includes soil, when it is solely used to cultivate goods (and not to enjoy the landscape), or materials such as oil and firewood, when they are used up by manufacturers and are no longer part of the final product. Since these objects do not lead to direct enjoyment, they do not have a direct value: their indirect value is derived from their contribution to the production of objects of the first and second classes.

Gossen argues that traditional economic theory is focused exclusively on the production of material objects, whereas attention should be directed towards their enjoyment. Therefore, immaterial objects should also receive attention, since they also provide enjoyment. He believed that the science of economics should be renamed the "doctrine of enjoyment", and the production of material and immaterial goods of the first and second classes should be examined from the point of view of the enjoyment that is generated by their consumption. The production of the third class of objects should be undertaken only insofar as it contributes to the production of objects of the first and second classes (Gossen 1854: 24–34). In contrast to the earlier cost-of-production or labour-value approaches of classical economics, Gossen considers value from the point of view of enjoyment: that is, from the demand side.

But the investigation of value does not stop here, since most objects can only be acquired by the exertion of human labour, which is unpleasant to some extent. Human labour is painful, and it increasingly fatigues the body the longer the exertion lasts. The value of the acquired objects must therefore be decreased by the estimation of that exertion. For Gossen, this exertion is always a form of movement: human force, guided by the knowledge of natural laws, moves parts of the exterior world in order to achieve the desired result. For instance, the cook moves the meat, the water, the butter and the salt into the pan, and then moves the pan over the fire, and the natural powers of the substances will then produce a roast dinner. Eating the roast dinner is also a form of movement, which will generate the enjoyment.

The unpleasantness of human exertion can be treated in a similar way to the pleasure of human enjoyment. Initially, after a period of rest, human exertion will produce pleasure. This pleasure of exertion will then be vulnerable to what was said before about pleasures: it will decrease over time. But whereas the consumption of a certain object will end when saturation has been reached, human exertion will continue even after the pleasure has sunk to zero, in order to acquire the objects of enjoyment. From this point on, exertion will become unpleasant; and the longer the exertion lasts, the more unpleasant the activity will become, until finally the person is exhausted and needs to rest. After a period of rest, the exertion can start over again. Given that human exertion can be discussed in a similar way to human enjoyment, we can represent both using similar graphs (see Figure 3.7).

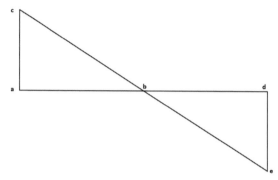

Figure 3.7 Decrease of enjoyment of human exertion over time.
Source: Gossen (1854: 14).

If human exertion takes place over time from point a to point d, then at first there will be enjoyment: initially, the line a–c. From then on, the enjoyment of the human exertion decreases, until we end up at point b, after which additional exertion will not generate additional enjoyment. While the consumption of a good would stop at this point, human exertion will continue, but from then on it will generate unpleasantness. This unpleasantness will grow for as long as the human exertion continues, and when we get to point d, the unpleasantness of the exertion is measured by the length d–e, which goes in the opposite direction to the initial enjoyment a–c (Gossen 1854: 34–7).

If human exertion were only to be seen as a form of enjoyment, then nobody would continue after point b, when saturation has set in. Labour is now defined as the human exertion beyond that point b, which is only undertaken because the product of the labour provides more pleasure than the human exertion provides unpleasantness. This can be illustrated by bringing the diagrams of enjoyment and exertion together.

Figure 3.8 represents the value of an object on top and the (un)pleasantness of human exertion at the bottom. It is clear that the human exertion will certainly continue until point h′, after which it becomes unpleasant. If we then make a "mirror copy" of the lower graph on the upper graph, we can see that labour should be exerted until point d, at which the additional pleasantness of the object is exactly equal to the additional unpleasantness of the human exertion (the length d–e for both). If we were to labour beyond point d, then the additional labour would become more unpleasant than the additional pleasure that we would derive from having more of the object. The maximum value has been achieved when the pain of the physical exertion to create additional objects becomes equal to the pleasure derived from these objects (Gossen 1854: 39).

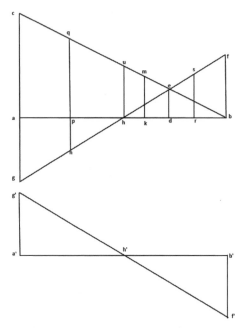

Figure 3.8 Decrease of enjoyment over time: consumption and human exertion.
Source: Gossen (1854: 39).

Consider, for example, a gardener who derives enjoyment from smelling his roses. The individual enjoyment derived from each additional rose will decline: he will derive a large amount of pleasure from smelling his first rose, but the additional enjoyment derived from, say, the 50th rose will be much smaller than that derived from the first rose. These roses are the product of his exertion. At first, this labour will be enjoyable, but after a while he will tire, which implies that continued human exertion will become ever more painful. But more labour will also generate more roses, although the additional enjoyment derived from each additional rose will decline. He will therefore continue to work as long as the additional exertion is less painful than smelling the additional rose is pleasurable. He will cease to work when the additional pleasure is smaller than the additional pain. Therefore, the pain of his last moment of time spent on gardening will be equal to the pleasure derived from smelling the last rose that he generates.

Human exertion, or labour, can take many different forms. However, the unpleasantness of human exertion – the fatigue of the human body – occurs irrespective of the specific object to which the labour is directed. We need to divide our limited labour power between different forms of occupation, which provide different forms of enjoyment, in such a way as to maximize the total amount of pleasure:

> In order to obtain the greatest enjoyment of life, man has to dis-
> tribute his time and energy over the realization of the various
> enjoyments in such a way, that the value of the last atom of every
> enjoyment equals the size of the pain, that would be caused to
> him if this atom were created in the last moment of his physical
> exertion.   (Gossen 1854: 45; my translation)

In other words, we maximize our pleasure when the last moments of time spent on each form of occupation are equally painful, and also equal to the pleasure derived from the last moments of time spent on the various forms of enjoyment.

Gossen illustrates this important conclusion with geometry, algebra and a numerical example, but we may also consider our gardening example. A gardener may devote his time to working on roses or on apple trees. Both activities are comparable in terms of human exertion. Suppose that the gardener derives more enjoyment from smelling the roses than from eating the apples. He would then initially devote his time to the roses. This has two consequences: he will get tired from his labour, but he will also increase the number of roses. When the gardener acquires more and more roses, the additional pleasure that he will derive from smelling yet another rose will decrease. He will clearly not work beyond the point where additional labour would be more painful than the additional roses would be pleasurable – as we have seen above, the labour will continue up to the point where the additional exertion would be equally painful as the additional product of the labour would be pleasurable.

But now there is an alternative: labouring on apple trees in order to taste apples. Given that the amount of additional pleasure derived from smelling a rose will decline when more roses are generated, at some point the pleasure of tasting the first apple may outweigh the pleasure of smelling yet another rose. The gardener will then start working on the apple trees, and increase the amount of apples. This will decrease the additional enjoyment derived from eating another apple, and at some point it may be more beneficial to allocate his labour to the roses again. He will continue to shift back and forth from apples to roses, thereby decreasing the additional pleasure derived from these products of his labour, but he will also get more tired. In the end, the pain of the last moment of time spent on gardening should be equal to the last "atom" of pleasure derived from either smelling the last rose or tasting the last apple. If this were not the case, then the gardener could increase his total pleasure by reallocating his labour.

All this implies that "value" is not something absolute, but something relative: it depends on the circumstances. For instance, gold is typically considered to be very valuable, but when Robinson Crusoe (who was shipwrecked and ended up alone on a desert island) found a nugget, he kicked it.

But even for one and the same person, the value of an object may be variable, as can be illustrated using the example of a collector. A collection will only provide full enjoyment for the collector when it is complete; the different components of the collection are therefore objects of the second class. Duplicates are to be removed from a collection, as they do not add to the enjoyment of the collection. This also implies that the value of the missing components increases when completion of the collection is within sight (Gossen 1854: 45–8).

Gossen summarizes the rules that need to be followed by an individual who wants to maximize his enjoyment over his lifetime: the number of enjoyments and their absolute size needs to be enlarged; his labour power and his skill need to be improved; the amount of labour required to produce the enjoyments needs to be decreased; and his labour needs to be spread out over different activities in accordance with these rules. These rules are, however, somewhat conflicting: we have multivariate functions that require us to use calculus. On the one hand, we want to use our labour in many different ways, in order to produce as many different enjoyments as possible. On the other hand, we improve our skill by directing our labour towards only a few possible enjoyments.

Even if we followed Gossen's rules and were able to exactly determine how much labour we should spend on all the various occupations, it would still be difficult for any individual to produce all possible enjoyments on his or her own. It follows that trade with specialized labourers is required if we want to maximize our total enjoyment. It is beneficial to trade if the object that I receive provides more additional enjoyment than the object that I give in exchange decreases my enjoyment. Since value is not something absolute, but something relative that depends on the circumstances, every act of exchange will change these circumstances and therefore change the value of the objects. When I receive more objects produced by somebody else, the additional enjoyment provided by yet another object will decrease, whereas the value of the object that I need to give in exchange will increase (because I have fewer of them). Ultimately, the exchange will remain beneficial until the value of the last "atom" of the received object becomes equal to the value of the last "atom" of the object given in exchange. It follows that division of labour and trade are very important. Every last "atom" of every object received will then ultimately provide the same amount of enjoyment (i.e. *net* enjoyment, since the pain of the human exertion required to obtain the object needs to be deducted). Gossen concludes: "Every individual thus receives exactly that share of the sum, which he can fairly claim" (Gossen 1854: 90; my translation).

Gossen tried to reform the field of economics by transforming it into a "doctrine of enjoyment" and by applying differential calculus. Unfortunately, his approach did not receive much attention from his contemporaries. His writings are remarkably similar to the political economy presented by Jevons, the first author of the "triumvirate" of the marginal revolution, whom we will discuss in the next chapter. As we will see, Jevons's analysis also starts with pleasures and pains, but his work is more centred around the notion of "utility", which describes the potential that an object has to provide pleasure for an individual consumer. The concept of "utility" had already been used by (French) economists, but it was Jules Dupuit who provided a clear definition that turned "utility" into a useful tool for economic analysis.

Dupuit on the measurement of utility

Dupuit (1844) wanted to investigate the utility of public works, such as roads, but economics was not very helpful since the concept of "utility" was not defined properly. The actual prices paid by society are not a good indicator of the utility society gains from its expenditure.

Suppose that France currently pays 500 million francs per annum for public roads. This does not imply that the utility of the French roads is equal to 500 million francs; it only indicates that the utility is *at least* 500 million francs: if it were less, society would not be willing to spend this amount. The 500 million francs is the cost of production, and cannot be taken as a measure of utility. If it were suddenly to become cheaper to produce roads, because of technological progress, then the cost of production would decrease but the utility of the roads would not change.

A further complication arises from the variability of utility:

> The utility of everything which is consumed varies according to the person consuming it. Nor is this all: each consumer himself attaches a different utility to the same thing according to the quantity which he can consume. (Dupuit 1844: 258)

For instance, the rich may be willing to pay 30 francs for a bottle of wine, some less rich people only 15 francs, whereas the poor might only be willing to pay 4 francs. Furthermore, individuals will decrease the amount they consume when the price increases: for instance, a purchaser may buy 100 bottles at 10 francs each but only 50 bottles at 15 francs each.

This reasoning can also be applied to public works. Suppose that an inhabitant consumes 1 hectolitre of water per day at a price of 50 francs. At such a high price, the water would only be used for essential purposes. If, due to technological progress, the price of the water were to drop to 20 francs, then this inhabitant will make a "profit" of 30 francs on his consumed hectolitre. But he may also increase his water consumption, since he can now use the water for purposes that he valued at above 20 francs but below 50 francs: he may, for instance, consume 4 hectolitres and use it to wash his car every day. At an even lower price of 10 francs per hectolitre he might demand 10 hectolitre to water his garden. If the price of water increases, perhaps because of taxation, inhabitants then reduce their consumed quantity: "Thus every product has a different utility not only for each consumer but for each of the wants for the satisfaction of which he uses it" (Dupuit 1844: 259).

Dupuit repeats Adam Smith's distinction between value in use and value in exchange (see chapter 1), but this requires a more precise definition that also takes the variability into account: "Political economy has to take as the measure of the utility of an object the maximum sacrifice which each consumer would be willing to make in order to acquire the object" (Dupuit 1844: 262).

The "absolute utility" of a product is determined by the amount of money that an individual would need to be paid in order to give up the consumption of a certain good. For example, a consumer may be willing to give up cleaning his car if he were given 30 francs. The "relative utility" is equal to the absolute utility less the purchase price. If the consumer were to get the product for free, then the relative utility would be equal to the absolute utility (30 francs in our example); if the purchase price were 20 francs, then the relative utility would only be 30 – 20 = 10 francs. If an individual must pay 20 francs for a certain product, then he also needs to give up consuming some other product to the tune of 20 francs, so the purchase price diminishes the utility for the individual. Therefore, if the purchase price is reduced, the (relative) utility for the individual increases; if the purchase price is increased, the (relative) utility for the individual falls. At the end of his article Dupuit represents his reasoning in geometrical form (shown in Figure 3.9).

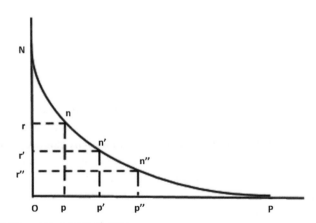

Figure 3.9 The measurement of utility.

Source: Dupuit (1844: 280).

On the x-axis we find the price p, and on the y-axis the corresponding quantity consumed by an individual, given the price. The length O–N is the quantity that would be consumed if the price were zero. At a price O–P or above nothing would be consumed. At the price O–p, the quantity n–p would be consumed; therefore, the utility for each of these units must be at least O–p, since otherwise the consumer would not be willing to purchase the quantity n–p at the price O–p.

In fact, it will be more for most of these units, which can be seen if we increase the price. If the price rose to O–p', then the lower quantity n'–p' would be consumed. This implies that the utility of these units must be at least O–p', since otherwise the consumer would not be willing to purchase the quantity n'–p' at the price O–p'. But these units would also be consumed at a lower price O–p (since n'–p' is smaller than n–p), and therefore at this lower purchase price they yielded a utility higher than the current purchase price. The "absolute utility" of n–p articles is therefore the area O-r-n-P, a "mixtilinear trapezium". In order to find the "relative utility" of n–p articles, we need to deduct the total purchase price for these articles, which is given by the rectangle O-r-n-p: the quantity n–p multiplied by the purchase price per unit O–p. The remainder is a "triangle" n–p–P. This relative utility will decline when the price increases, but less rapidly; if the price decreases, then the relative utility will increase, but more rapidly – this corresponds to the shortening or stretching of the "triangle". Dupuit concludes his essay with a plea for the use of mathematics in economics:

> In presenting, in this note, some of the principles of our science in this particular form it was our wish to try and make clear how great would be the advantages of an alliance with mathematics, despite the anathema which economists of all times have pronounced against the latter… Not only do the symbols and drawings of mathematics give body and form to abstract ideas and thereby call the senses to the aid of man's intellectual power, but its formulae take hold of these ideas, modify them, and transform them, and bring to light everything that is true, right and precise in them, without forcing the mind to follow all the motions of a wheelwork the course of which has been established once for all.   (Dupuit 1844: 283)

The main contribution of Dupuit is that he turned the concept of "utility", which is inherently variable, into a useful tool for economic analysis. The absolute utility of public works, such as roads, is determined by society's willingness to pay for these roads. If the cost of production of the roads, which is society's purchase price, exceeds this absolute utility, then society would not be willing to build the roads. If the absolute utility is exactly equal to the cost of production (or society's purchase price), then society would build the road but there would be no (relative) utility left. If the cost of production (and therefore society's purchase price) were to go down, then the absolute utility would be higher than the purchase price and society would be left with relative utility.

The economic theory of Jevons, which we will investigate in the next chapter, starts with an analysis of pleasures and pains, similar to the writings of Gossen. He then defines the concept of "utility" in a similar way to Dupuit. Jevons defines labour as a painful exertion and therefore as a "disutility", which again echoes Gossen's work. As soon as he turns his attention to the theory of rent, discussed in chapter 2, he notices a similarity between his utility theory (the demand side) and marginal productivity theory (the supply side). This similarity, which is worked out further by authors such as Marshall and Clark (see chapter 7), will eventually bring us to what is known today as "microeconomic theory".

4

Jevons: mathematics, mechanics and marginalism

William Stanley Jevons is the first main author of the marginal revolution. At first sight his work is very similar to that of Gossen. Jevons acknowledges the importance of Gossen's writings: "Gossen has completely anticipated me as regards the general principles and method of the theory of Economics" (Jevons 1879: xxxviii). There are also, however, some substantial differences between the two.

First of all, Jevons's analysis departs explicitly from the moral philosophy of Jeremy Bentham (1748–1832), called "utilitarianism" (see below). Furthermore, Jevons puts an even stronger emphasis on mathematics than Gossen, and in particular on calculus. Finally, Jevons goes beyond Gossen when he realizes that the theory of rent, which we discussed in chapter 2, is "a theory of a distinctively mathematical character, which seems to give a clue to the correct mode of treating the whole science" (Jevons 1879: vi). In other words, Jevons realized that the theory of rent could be transformed into a general theory of economics. This insight was worked out further by Alfred Marshall and John Bates Clark, as we will investigate in our chapter 7.

Jevons's main work in economic theory, *The Theory of Political Economy*, was published for the first time in 1871. He had already presented a "Notice of a General Mathematical Theory of Political Economy" at a conference of the British Association for the Advancement of Science (now known as the British Science Association) in 1862, and in 1866 he published an article titled "A brief account of a general mathematical theory of political economy" in the *Journal of the Statistical Society*. These works did not, however, receive a lot of attention. The second edition of Jevons's *Theory of Political Economy* (TPE), which appeared in 1879, was a substantial revision and extension, and in what follows we will refer to this text.

Jevons argues that "political economy" has to be replaced by the more convenient term "economics", as it is similar to the names of other branches of human knowledge, and as several important economists (including Marshall) were already using this concept (Jevons 1879: xiv).[1] In his concluding sentences, Jevons makes clear that he wants to do more than just change the name of the field:

> When at length a true system of Economics comes to be established, it will be seen that that able but wrong-headed man, David Ricardo, shunted the car of Economic Science on to a wrong line, a line, however, on which it was further urged towards confusion by his equally able and wrong-headed admirer John Stuart Mill.
>
> (Jevons 1879: lvii)

Starting from his mathematical agenda, Jevons wants to reconstruct classical political economy using the central notion of "utility".[2]

In what follows, we will first examine Jevons's mathematical agenda further. We will then move on to his theory of utility. Thereafter, we will investigate Jevons's theory of exchange, which describes how individuals can increase their levels of utility through market exchange. Finally, we will look at his theories of labour, rent and capital, which pave the way for a unified view of economic theory using the theory of rent.

Mathematics and calculus

A very important aspect of Jevons's economics is its mathematical agenda. Given that economics deals with quantities, it simply must be mathematical. For instance, the laws of supply and demand deal with quantities supplied and demanded, and therefore they are mathematical.

---

1. Remarkably, Jevons did not change the title of his book (*The Theory of Political Economy*) for the second edition: "Though employing the new name [*Economics*] in the text, it was obviously undesirable to alter the title-page of the book" (Jevons 1879: xiv).
2. For a discussion of Jevons's attempted reconstruction of economics, see Mosselmans (2007).

Classical economists do not use mathematical symbols to explain the laws of supply and demand, but that does not imply that these laws are not mathematical. On the contrary, using appropriate mathematical symbols would make economics much more precise. Ordinary language is insufficient to describe complex relations between quantities, and therefore leads to an imperfect science. The appropriate branch of mathematics is differential calculus, as it considers infinitely small quantities (Jevons 1879: 3–5). Jevons: "In short, I do not write for mathematicians, nor as a mathematician, but as an economist wishing to convince other economists that their science can only be satisfactorily treated on an explicitly mathematical basis" (Jevons 1879: xiii). Jevons points out that, due to the dominance of the Ricardian school, English economists have ignored the works of French, English, German and Italian authors who treated economics in a mathematical way. In order to assist his English colleagues, Jevons drew up a list of mathematical–economic writings, which was published in the *Journal of the London Statistical Society* in 1878, and forwarded it to several leading economists, subsequently updating it and adding it to a second edition of TPE as an appendix.

Dupuit was on the list for having clearly defined the notion of "utility". As we saw in the previous chapter, not only does the utility of a good vary between different individuals, but it also varies for the same individual according to the quantity that he can consume. Jevons recognizes Dupuit's importance:

> He establishes, in fact, a theory of the *gradation of utility*, beautifully and perfectly expounded by means of geometrical diagrams, and this theory is undoubtedly coincident in essence with that contained in this [Jevons's] book. He does not, however, follow his ideas out in an algebraic form. (Jevons 1879: xxxi)

One of the other works on the list was Cournot's *Researches* (1838), which we will discuss briefly in the next chapter as it had a major influence on the economics of Walras. According to Jevons, Cournot should occupy "a remarkable position" in the history of economics, not so much for his theoretical perspectives (since there is no theory of utility in Cournot's writings), but rather for his mathematical treatment of supply and demand.

Demand for a good is written in a functional form $D = F(p)$, which simply means that the function F expresses that quantity demanded (D) varies when the price (p) changes. Cournot's method is then to assume that some simple conditions of this function conform to experience: for instance, experience shows that quantity demanded goes up when the price goes down, and this mathematical relationship is expressed by the formula. According to Jevons, Cournot's approach to economics is the correct one: we start from simple relations that we express in mathematical form, then we manipulate these formulas until we finally achieve more precise results than ordinary language ever could (Jevons 1879: xxx–xxxiv). Jevons combines Cournot's mathematical approach with the theory of utility.

The theory of utility

Jevons's theory of utility departs from Bentham's utilitarianism. Bentham was a moral philosopher who approached ethical problems as a "consequentialist": the moral value of human actions must be evaluated by the consequences of these actions.

For instance, we could evaluate whether the establishment of a public car park would be a good thing or not. We would list all the consequences of creating the car park. Obviously, the car park would be beneficial for car owners. It would also be beneficial for the shop owners in the neighbourhood of the car park, as it would attract more customers. On the other hand, the people who live in the area may experience more traffic and therefore more air pollution. In order to undertake a cost–benefit analysis of this public car park, we need to express all these consequences – positive for some but negative for others – in terms of pleasures and pains. The car park will then be established if the total amount of pleasure gained by the car park (for car owners and shopkeepers) exceeds the total amount of pain caused by the car park (for local inhabitants). The ultimate goal is to achieve "the greatest happiness of the greatest number".[3] Bentham's approach to the evaluation of human actions is transformed by Jevons into an economic theory.

---

3. See, for example, Driver (2007: 40–79) for more about utilitarianism.

Jevons describes his economic theory as "the mechanics of utility and self-interest" (Jevons 1879: 23). This requires, first of all, a theory of pleasure and pain, seen as quantities. Borrowing from Bentham, the value of a feeling (either a pleasure or a pain) depends on its intensity, its duration, its remoteness and its certainty.[4] Every feeling has two dimensions: namely, its intensity and the time that it lasts. Two other properties, remoteness and certainty, further affect the quantity of this feeling. A future feeling may already be anticipated in the present, and this anticipation will be stronger the less remote in time this feeling will occur: "The intensity of present anticipated feeling must, to use a mathematical expression, be *some function of the future actual feeling and of the intervening time*, and it must increase as we approach the moment of realisation" (Jevons 1879: 37). Obviously, this anticipation will also be stronger if the future feeling is expected to appear with more certainty.

For example, we all know that a toothache can be very annoying. The pain can vary in intensity. The pain may last for only a very short time, e.g. when we consume ice cream, but it may also be a continuous pain that lasts for days. It is clear that the value of the feeling, pain in this case, will increase when it is more intense, and also when it lasts longer. In order to get rid of this pain, we may decide to visit the dentist. Most people do not enjoy visiting the dentist. Extraction of the offending tooth may cause intense pain, but only during a relatively short period in time. After the treatment the pain will be relieved. Therefore, most people would be willing to endure a short intense pain at the dentist's in order to be relieved of the chronic toothache that lasts a long time, even if, at any single moment during that time, the chronic pain is less intense than the pain felt during the extraction.

Remoteness plays a role as well: I may not be worried about a visit to the dentist that is planned for next month, but I will feel more anxious as the

---

4. Bentham considers three additional circumstances: fecundity (the chance that a feeling will be followed by a similar feeling), purity (the chance that a feeling will not be followed by a feeling of the opposite kind) and extent (the number of persons affected). These additional circumstances are ignored by Jevons: "These three last circumstances are of high importance as regards the theory of morals; but they will not enter into the more simple and restricted problem which we attempt to solve in Economics" (Jevons 1879: 31).

date of the visit approaches. It will also be easier to endure the treatment if we anticipate that afterwards we will be relieved of the pain. Certainty is also important: would we visit the dentist if we did not know for certain that he would relieve our pain? These four properties also indicate why it is so difficult to stop smoking. The consumption of tobacco causes intense pleasure immediately, and it might only cause pain (disease) in the remote future, and even this will not happen with certainty.

These properties allow us to make simple calculations: two days of severe toothache count for twice as much as one day of severe toothache, and the short intense pain of the dentist's treatment counts for less than the chronic pain that I have endured for a week. However, the intensity of a feeling will normally vary from moment to moment, so we would need to make calculations of feeling for every moment in time.

Suppose that eating an apple gives us pleasure for about an hour: a greater amount in the beginning, when we are very hungry, but almost nothing of the pleasure remains an hour later, when we may have become hungry again. In order to find out the total amount of pleasure generated by consuming the apple, we would need to consider every minute of the hour separately and then add up the pleasure generated for every minute. If the pleasure were the same during every minute, then the total amount of pleasure during one hour would simply be equal to 60 times the pleasure generated in each minute. But the amount of pleasure typically decreases over time, as in our example with the apple. We could, of course, subdivide the time period further: into seconds, for instance. Theoretically, we could look at the amount of feeling for only a tiny amount of time, which becomes infinitely small if we continue to make the periods shorter. It is here that calculus comes in, as this form of mathematics deals with infinitely small quantities. Jevons illustrates his reasoning with a set of graphs (Jevons 1879: 30–9). The amount of time is measured on the x-axis, whereas the intensity of feeling is placed on the y-axis.

In Figure 4.1, we have subdivided our time period (from m to n) into equal smaller periods and assumed that the amount of feeling remained constant during each small period. This gives us several rectangles – one for each small period – the area of which provides us with the quantity of feeling generated during that small period. By adding up all these areas we get the total quantity of feeling.

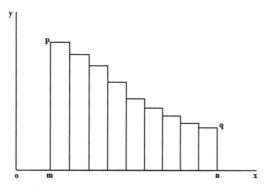

Figure 4.1 Intensity of feeling during a time period, subdivided into smaller equal periods.
Source: Jevons (1879: 33).

As in the example of the apple, in the graph we see that the amount of feeling decreases over time. If we now make these time periods infinitely small, then we get a continuous function, as represented in Figure 4.2. In this case, the amount of feeling is equal to the area under the curve, bound by the vertical lines that indicate the first and last moment of the time period under consideration (from m to n). It is remarkable to see the similarity between Jevons's and Gossen's diagrams.

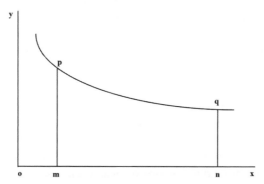

Figure 4.2 Intensity of feeling during a time period: continuous case.
Source: Jevons (1879: 34).

An individual will usually achieve pleasure or eliminate pain through the consumption of a good or the performance of an action. Jevons introduces the term "commodity" to discuss this matter: "By a *commodity* we shall understand any object, substance, action or service, which can afford pleasure or ward off pain" (Jevons 1879: 41). Any object that can serve our purposes is a "commodity", and the abstract quality whereby this commodity can serve our purposes is called "utility".

It is important to understand that "utility" is not an intrinsic quality of the commodity, but a circumstance of things arising out of their relation to a person's requirements. For instance, water can provide a lot of utility in the desert, but it will provide negative utility, or "disutility", when it continues to rain in an area that is already flooded. A hungry person will usually derive a lot of utility from a steak, unless this person is allergic to meat, in which case forcing him or her to consume the steak will cause disutility.

Utility is also not proportional to commodity: the more units of a certain good are in my possession, the less additional utility will be provided by an additional unit of that same good. Typically, the amount of additional utility will decrease when more units of the commodity are consumed. The first glass of water will provide a lot of utility when I am very thirsty, the second will also provide utility, given that I am still thirsty, but to a lesser extent than the first glass. The seventh glass will probably provide hardly any additional utility, and since drinking too much water may lead to water poisoning, at some point it will deliver disutility rather than additional utility.

We can illustrate this property with the same graphs as above, but now we measure the amount of commodity on the x-axis (expressed in terms of units), and the amount of utility generated on the y-axis. This could be a quantity of food: bread, for instance. In Figure 4.1 we could use a loaf of bread as a unit, or simply a slice of bread, but in each case the additional utility generated by consumption will decrease when more units are consumed. Theoretically, we could consider bread crumbs as a unit, and then arrive at the continuous function (Figure 4.2). The total utility is found by the area under the graph, bound by the two vertical lines, as before.

More interesting, however, is the degree of utility, which is the amount of utility generated by every increment. An increment of a good is an increase in the quantity of that good, by consuming an additional unit – in the case of bread, it could be a loaf, a slice or even a crumb of bread. The degree of utility tells us by how much the total utility of the bread increases when we consume an additional unit. The degree of utility is basically the change in utility divided by the length of the increment: for instance, the increase in utility caused by having another slice of bread (which is the increment).

If we make this increment infinitely small (a crumb of bread), to arrive at the continuous case, then we can use differential calculus to explore the utility theory algebraically. If utility is represented by u and the increase in utility by du, and if bread is represented by x and the increment of bread by dx, then the degree of utility for any increment is found by du/dx, which is the first derivative of utility to quantity of commodity. The final degree of utility is then the utility generated by the final or last increment (loaf, slice or crumb of bread). Contemporary economists call this the "marginal utility", or the utility at the margin – we will also use this concept in what follows. The marginal utility of bread is equal to the additional utility generated by consuming the last loaf, slice or crumb of bread. Jevons (1879: 57) formulates what is now typically called Gossen's first law or the law of diminishing marginal utility: "The degree of utility varies with the quantity of commodity, and ultimately decreases as that quantity increases". In other words, the marginal utility of bread decreases when more bread is consumed. This also works in the opposite direction: the marginal utility of bread will increase when less bread is consumed.

A further complication arises when a certain commodity can be used in different ways. For instance, you may consume more bread, but you may instead use the bread to feed the birds. If you like birds because they make your garden more lively, and if feeding bread to the birds attracts more birds, then giving bread to the birds will also increase your utility (as it makes your garden more lively). A rational consumer wants to maximize his utility and must therefore decide how much bread to eat and how much to use to feed the birds. As a general rule, the marginal utility of bread must be equal for both purposes. If the last unit of bread (loaf, slice or crumb) provides less additional utility when consumed than if it were given to the birds, then I could increase my total utility by eating less bread and giving more of it to the birds.

Gossen's first law of diminishing marginal utility (see above) applies: when I eat less bread, the marginal utility of bread consumption will increase; when I give more bread to the birds, the marginal utility of bread used for feeding the birds will decrease. As long as the marginal utility of consuming bread is smaller than the marginal utility of using the bread to feed the birds, I will increase my total utility by eating less bread and giving more to the birds. If the marginal utility for both purposes is the same, then I cannot increase my total utility by redistributing the bread over the two purposes. It follows that our utility is maximized if the utility generated by the last unit of bread is equal for every use that is made of it: in this case, consuming or feeding the birds. No further improvements in utility are possible if the last loaf, slice or crumb of bread that I eat gives me exactly the same amount of additional utility as using the last loaf, slice or crumb to feed the birds. This is now commonly known as Gossen's second law: if a commodity can be used for different ways, then the marginal utility for every purpose must be equal (Jevons 1879: 49–66).

The theory of exchange

So far we have only considered simple acts of consumption that provide utility to the consumer. In a market economy, individual market partici-pants can increase their utility through the exchange of goods. The theory of exchange is therefore at the core of economics.

Gains in exchange can be made when different individuals value com-modities differently. If one person owns a lot of bread but only a little bit of butter, and another person owns very little bread but a lot of butter, then both of them would increase their utility by exchanging bread for butter (and butter for bread). Exchange value is not a thing, but a ratio, as it expresses how many units of a certain good can be exchanged against a certain amount of units of another good. Jevons prefers the term "ratio of exchange" rather than the ambiguous term "value" to discuss the exchange of two commodities.

The process of exchange requires a medium in which this exchange takes place, which Jevons calls a "market". A market is defined as "two or more persons dealing in two or more commodities, whose stocks of those com-modities and intentions of exchange are known to all" (Jevons 1879: 92). Therefore, the definition of the market presupposes the existence of perfect information: whoever does not know the conditions of supply and demand cannot be considered part of the market. The owner of the bread knows how much butter (and how little bread) the other person has and how much butter the other person would be willing to give up in exchange for bread. The owner of the butter has exactly the same information about the owner of the bread. A market can only be theoretically perfect when all traders have this perfect information. Jevons calls these traders "trading bodies", which can be individuals (as in our bread and butter example) but also aggregates of individuals such as nations.

Given the existence of such a market, and if a commodity is homogeneous in quality, then at any point in time all portions of the commodity must be exchanged at the same ratio. If the bread and the butter are homogeneous in quality within a certain market, then a certain amount of bread must always be exchanged for the same amount of butter. Nowadays this is known as "the law of one price", but Jevons calls it the "law of indifference": "in the same open market, at any one moment, there cannot be two prices for the same kind of article" (Jevons 1879: 99). If the prevailing price for a computer is €500, then nobody will be able to sell a computer at €501, provided that the computers are uniform in quality and that everybody has perfect information (which is a prerequisite of the definition of a market, as we saw above). Consumers will simply switch to the cheaper seller.

Of course, prices fluctuate all the time, because transactions are taking place continuously. These transactions will change the conditions of supply and demand, as the market participants will have more or less of the goods after the exchange has been completed. This would require studying exchange as a dynamic process. But treating exchange as a dynamic process would make it very complicated, and therefore, at least in the first instance, exchange should be studied as a purely static problem. In its simplest form, we can consider a market with two people, each in possession of a certain number of units of two different goods. Starting from this static situation, we can allow the two individuals to exchange goods, in order to increase their utility. After the process of exchange has been completed, we arrive at a new equilibrium, or a new static situation. A static approach investigates and compares the two equilibria rather than trying to model the dynamic shift from the initial equilibrium towards the final equilibrium.

Given that there can be only one price in the market, "the last increments in an act of exchange must be exchanged in the same ratio as the whole quantities exchanged" (Jevons 1879: 102). In other words, the ratio of exchange between two goods will be equal to the ratio of exchange between the last increments of these goods.

Jevons illustrates the process of exchange with two trading bodies that are exchanging corn for beef (and beef for corn). Suppose that one trading body owns only corn, whereas a second trading body possesses only beef. It is reasonable to suppose that the utility of the first trading body could increase if it were to exchange some of its corn for beef – an exchange that would at the same time increase the utility of the second trading body.

Suppose that, at a certain static moment, 10 pounds of corn would exchange for one pound of beef. If the first trading body finds 10 pounds of corn less useful than one pound of beef, it will be eager to engage in a process of exchange. If the second trading body finds 10 pounds of corn more useful than one pound of beef, it will also be willing to exchange. Exchange will go on as long as both parties find this beneficial. However, as we know from Gossen's first law, the marginal utility, or the utility of the last increment of a good, will go down when more units of the good are in the possession of the trading body. So by giving up corn in exchange for beef, the first trading body will have less corn and more beef after the exchange, and therefore the marginal utility of corn will increase, whereas the marginal utility of beef will decrease.

Suppose that the first trading body considers 15 pounds of corn to have equal utility to one pound of beef. It would therefore be willing to exchange at the prevailing price (10 pounds of corn for one pound of beef). However, after this exchange the relative valuation will have changed – given that the first trading body now has less corn and more beef, it may consider one pound of beef to be equally useful to only 14 pounds of corn. This is still above the ratio of exchange; so exchange will continue and the relative valuation will change once more. This process will continue until the ratio of exchange becomes equal to the relative valuations, for both trading bodies, as from this point on no further gains in utility can be made through exchange. If 10 pounds of corn are valued equal to one pound of beef by both trading bodies, and if 10 pounds of corn also exchange for one pound of beef, then exchange would not make sense given that utility would not increase (Jevons 1879: 103–4).

This can also be seen as an application of Gossen's second law. If a consumer faces a choice between spending an additional penny on corn or on beef, then the penny will be spent on that good which provides the most utility. Hence, if I derive more utility from spending a penny on corn than on beef, then it would make sense to consume more corn and less beef. If my last penny spent on corn or on beef provided me with the same amount of utility, then I would be indifferent between buying corn or beef. Hence, in equilibrium, the last penny spent on both corn and beef should provide me with the same amount of utility. In conclusion, we need a perfect market that automatically establishes a new equilibrium through exchange, which will maximize utility for all market participants.

The theories of labour, rent and capital

Now that Jevons has considered the theory of utility and exchange, he turns to the determination of the share of the value of the final product that goes to the owners of the means of production: labour, rent and capital. Given that each final product is made by using these resources, their owners must receive an appropriate reward. Labourers get paid wages for their labour, the owners of land receive rent, and the owners of capital receive profits. As we saw before, for classical economists this distribution was prior to exchange. The natural value of a good is equal to its cost of production in the worst possible circumstances. As we saw in chapter 2, rent is zero in these worst possible circumstances. The rent of land does not therefore enter into the natural value of the final product, as all goods are exchanged at the same price, regardless of whether they were produced in good or bad circumstances.

Jevons realizes that this is an application of the "law of one price", which we discussed above. Since rent has been eliminated as a differential surplus, the value of the final product must be distributed between wages and profits. Jevons rejects this conclusion for two reasons. First of all because the value of the final product cannot be determined beforehand: it is established in a process of exchange, as we explained above. But more importantly, there is no such thing as a natural wage rate. Wage rates tend to vary a lot, and it is impossible to determine what the subsistence level might be. Therefore, there is no way to clearly determine which part goes to wages and which part is left for profits (Jevons 1879: 291–2).

Value is only established in the process of exchange, and therefore the issue of distribution must be considered after the exchange has been completed.[5] As we will explain below, Jevons realized that the theory of rent can also be used to determine the share that goes to wages and to profits. In TPE, the theories of labour, rent and capital are discussed successively.

Jevons (1879:183) defines labour as "any painful exertion of mind or body undergone partly or wholly with a view to future good". Labourers are paid wages for their work, and these wages are used to purchase goods on the market. These goods will provide pleasure, and therefore utility, to the labourers. Labour can be pleasurable, but only to a limited extent. Typically, labourers will work beyond the limit at which labour is still agreeable, given their willingness to acquire future good. Generally, labour becomes increasingly painful the longer it goes on. What is of interest is the point at which the exertion stops. The exertion stops because the labourer's pain outweighs the benefits he derives from consuming wage goods. This can be illustrated with the following graph (Figure 4.3), which is again very similar to Gossen's graph that we discussed in the previous chapter.

The lower curve describes the pleasure (or pain) of ordinary labour. The x-axis represents the number of hours of work, and on the y-axis we read the corresponding pain (or pleasure). The first moments of work are typically hard: "At the moment of commencing labour it is usually more irksome than when the mind and body are well bent to the work" (Jevons 1879: 187). Therefore, between points a and b the pleasure derived from the labour itself is negative. Between points b and c the labour becomes pleasurable. After point c the energy of the labourer gets exhausted, and the pleasure becomes negative (and therefore turns into pain) and continues to decline as the working day is prolonged.

---

5. When comparing TPE (1871/1879) and his earlier "A brief account ..." (1866), it is interesting to note that the theories of labour and of rent changed their positions in Jevons's theoretical framework. Whereas "A brief account..." treats labour and rent before the theory of exchange, these matters are discussed after the part on exchange in TPE. This issue has been investigated by Michael V. White (1991), who argues convincingly that Jevons initially approached the problem of economics from within a classical framework, but that he failed to determine the profit rate that way. Jevons then realized that the theory of rent, through its application of the law of one price, may provide a general explanation for the rewards given to the means of production: wages for labour, rent for land and profits or interest for capital.

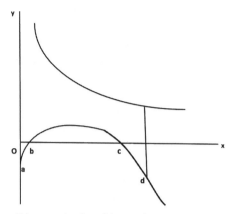

Figure 4.3 Disutility of labour and utility of the produce.
Source: Jevons (1879: 187).

The upper curve represents the diminishing marginal utility of the produce of the labour, typically given to the labourer in the form of wages. There are then two effects of the prolongation of the working day: labour becomes more painful and, at the same time, the marginal utility of the produce decreases. This decrease in the marginal utility of the produce is explained by Gossen's first law of diminishing marginal utility, but also because labourers become less productive in later hours compared with earlier hours at work.

Until point d, the marginal utility of the produce exceeds the painfulness (or the marginal disutility) of the labour, and therefore the labourer would like to work. Beyond point d the labourer would not like to work, since the additional utility that she gets from working is lower than the additional pain (or disutility) of the physical exertion. The labourer would therefore like to offer labour up to point d, in which case the marginal utility of the produce is exactly equal to the marginal disutility of the labour.

The labourer will continue to work an additional hour as long as the benefit derived from the labour (the wage) gives more pleasure than the labour provides pain. In equilibrium, the marginal disutility of labour will be equal to the marginal utility of the produce. Hence, this margin will determine how many hours will be worked. If a labourer could divide her time over producing two different objects, then clearly she would spend an additional hour on that good which yields the highest additional utility (provided that the labour bestowed on both goods was equally painful). Hence, the utility derived from the last hour of labour spent on each of the two goods must be equal – this is actually an application of Gossen's second law.

When combining the theories of exchange and labour, Jevons first notes that exchange value is typically proportional to the cost of production (mainly labour): the price of a good tends to increase when its production becomes more costly. However, this does not imply that we should look out for a cost of production theory of value, as in classical political economy. The exchange value will be determined by the costs of production of *the last portions added* (Jevons 1879: 181–205). This can be illustrated and explained with the theory of rent, which Jevons considers next.

Jevons (1879: 228) states that "the general correctness of the views put forth in preceding chapters derives probability from their close resemblance to the theory of rent, as it has been accepted by English writers for nearly a century". In particular, the theory of rent rests on the law of one price. If there are different qualities of land, then more fertile land will yield more produce than less fertile land, given that all commodities are sold at the same price. Nobody would be willing to pay more for, say, a potato because it was produced in less fertile circumstances. And since more fertile land will yield more potatoes than less fertile land (given the same inputs of labour and capital), the final value of its output will be higher.

We saw in chapter 2 that the existence of land of different qualities is a first source of rent, which we called "extensive rent". Furthermore, when more units of labour and capital are applied to a piece of land, the produce will not increase proportionally. Again as we saw in chapter 2, there are diminishing returns in agriculture. If this were not the case, then we could feed the entire world using one piece of land if only we applied a sufficient amount of labour and capital. These diminishing returns in agriculture are a second source of rent, which we called "intensive rent". The theory of rent can be illustrated with a diagram (Figure 4.4), which represents the labour that is applied to land of a certain given quality. The x-axis represents the work hours, whereas on the y-axis we read the marginal product of that labour, i.e. the additional produce generated by that amount of labour. Since there are diminishing returns to agriculture, it is no surprise to see that this is a downward-sloping curve.

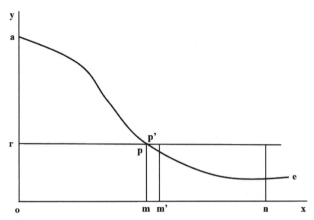

Figure 4.4 Graphical representation of the theory of rent.
Source: Jevons (1879: 238).

The owner of the land will hire additional labour as long as his marginal benefit (the value of the additional produce) exceeds the marginal cost (the wage of the labourer). If the marginal benefit exceeds the marginal cost, then the owner of the land will hire more labour; if the marginal benefit is below the marginal cost, then he will reduce his labour force. Hence, in equilibrium (as economists like to say), the value of the produce of the last unit of labour (the marginal benefit) will be equal to the wage (the marginal cost).

Starting from any static point in time, we can therefore find the wage rate (the marginal cost) by identifying the value of the additional product of labour (the marginal benefit). Suppose that the amount of labour o–m has been applied to the land: the corresponding marginal product m–p (which is identical to the length o–r) will then be equal to the wage rate. But given the law of one price, all hours of labour will receive the same wage, including the hours of labour that yielded a marginal benefit higher than m–p. Since there are diminishing returns in agriculture, this is the case for all points that lie to the left of m. A straight line can then be drawn from p to r, which represents the wage rate paid to all units of labour. Hence, the total wages paid to the labourers are equal to o–m (the number of hours worked) multiplied by the wage rate o–r, which corresponds to the area o–r–p–m. The area above this rectangle, r–a–p, is then the rent that can be charged by the owner of the land. It is clear that the difference between the

89

marginal product and the wage is very high for the first units of labour, but then declines to become zero for the last unit of labour expended (Jevons 1879: 228–40). If labour and land are the only means of production, then all units of labour will be rewarded at a wage rate that is equal to the marginal product of the last unit of labour that is employed. All earlier units of labour will yield a higher marginal product, and this surplus product will be given to the owner of the land as a rent income.

As we saw in previous chapters, modern economies use capital as a third factor of production, in addition to labour and land. Therefore, the theory of capital concludes Jevons's theory of political economy. His views on capital are not very different from those of earlier writers, which we discussed in our previous chapters. It usually takes some time before a final product is ready and sold at the market, and in the interim the labourers must survive on wages that are paid out of the capital stock. Furthermore, labourers require tools, which also need to be purchased by their employer. Capital is thus concerned with time, as it consists in "the aggregate of those commodities which are required for sustaining labourers of any kind or class engaged in work" (Jevons 1879: 242).

In some industries this capital needs to remain invested for a considerable amount of time. For instance, a vineyard remains unproductive for at least three years, and it may take six years or more before gold is found in a new gold mine. The labourers obviously need to be supported during those years in which no produce is generated. Furthermore, since the labourers require tools, these need to be produced beforehand: "Capital simply allows us to expend labour in advance" (Jevons 1879: 245).

Given that capital can be applied to any industry – you can borrow capital from a bank – it follows that the rate of interest, which is the reward for capital, must be uniform. This is, again, a direct application of the law of one price (Jevons 1879: 264–5). The interest of capital is "the rate of increase of the produce divided by the whole produce" (Jevons 1879: 267). This can best be illustrated with a numerical example. Suppose that I have a capital stock of €100 at the beginning of the year, which I invest in a certain business. This means that I buy tools and machinery, hire labourers and rent a piece of land. These means of production allow me to produce a certain amount of goods, which are brought to the market and sold. A year later my tools and machinery have worn out, so they have "depreciated" in value. The amount of depreciation needs to be deducted from the value of my capital stock. I have also paid wages to the labourers and rent to the owner of the land. But I also made a profit, and this profit has been added to my capital stock. If the total value of my capital stock is now €110, then I made a profit of €10, and the interest of capital is equal to (€110 – €100)/(€100) = 10 per cent. This rate must be the same in all industries, since otherwise the "invisible hand" would spring into action and capital would shift from one sector to another. The "law of one price" prevails.

If the labourer is his own capitalist and also the owner of the land, then there would be no difference between wages, profits and rent: these would all simply be income for the labourer. When the ownership of these means of production is separate, then the labourer is paid at a wage rate that is equal to the marginal product of his labour, i.e. the additional value generated by the last hour of work. The earlier hours of work yield a higher product, and this surplus product must be distributed between the profit for the owner of the capital and the rent for the owner of the land. Jevons writes in his concluding remarks that "the wages of a working man are ultimately coincident with what he produces, after the deduction of rent, taxes, and the interest of capital" (Jevons 1879: 292). This refers back to what Jevons said at the beginning of TPE: the theory of rent gives us a clue about how economic theory should be treated in general. Every factor of production (labour, land and capital) will be paid at a rate that is equal to its marginal product, which is the additional product generated by the "last" unit, or by the unit that is used in the least productive circumstances. Ultimately – and therefore in the long run and on average across every branch of employment – the labourer would receive the marginal product of his labour as wages, the land owner would receive the marginal product of his land as rent, and the residual, which would be equal to the marginal product of capital, would determine the profit rate.

Jevons does not, however, work out this idea further – this will be left to later authors such as Marshall and Clark, whom we will investigate in chapter 7. Nor does he develop his system into a general equilibrium theory, like his contemporary Walras (1874), as we will discuss in the next chapter.

5

Walras and general equilibrium theory

Léon Walras wrote his most important work, *Elements of Pure Economics or the Theory of Social Wealth* (EPE, 1874), at around the same time as Jevons published *Theory of Political Economy*. At first sight, the theories of Jevons and Walras appear to be very similar. Jevons describes the process of exchange, which allows trading bodies to exchange commodities in order to maximize their utility; in equilibrium, the ratio of exchange between two goods will be equal to the relative valuations for both trading bodies. Walras calls this the "condition of maximum satisfaction", and he recognizes that his analysis is very similar to that of Jevons. Moreover, Walras praises Jevons's use of mathematics.[1]

However, Walras's work does not depart from Bentham's theory of utilitarianism. More importantly, Walras goes beyond Jevons in his description of the entire economy. For Jevons, the process of exchange takes place between two trading bodies that are exchanging two goods. He does of course know that there are more than two trading bodies and more than two goods in modern markets, but his analysis remains restricted to this simple case. Walras, by contrast, aims to develop a mathematical model that describes the economy as a whole.

---

1. In the preface of a later edition of his *Elements of Pure Economics*, Walras stresses that he only heard about Jevons's *Theory of Political Economy* after his own book was written and almost completely printed. Jevons did not therefore influence the development of Walras's thought, despite TPE having been published a few years before EPE. Walras also recognizes Gossen's priority as far as the utility curve is concerned. He also mentions Carl Menger from the University of Vienna (see Chapter 6), who, independently of other authors, stressed the importance of marginal utility (which Walras calls *rareté* as we will see below). Walras refers to his father Auguste Walras as a major influence on his fundamental principles of economics, and to Cournot for using calculus of functions (Walras 1874: 35–7).

We saw in the previous chapter that every act of exchange alters the conditions of supply and demand, since after the exchange the trading bodies will hold more or less of each commodity. This will in turn affect their relative valuations, and therefore the ratio of exchange or the market price. However, a different price for one good may also have implications for another. For instance, we all know that the price of airline flights tends to increase when the price of oil goes up. This is obvious, because oil is an important input for the airline flight industry. But even goods that do not seem to be interconnected may influence each other. For instance, housing is usually a large share of the budget of any consumer. When the price of housing increases, consumers may then have to cut their spending on nearly all other goods. Walras wants to set up a mathematical model that deals with these forms of multi-commodity exchange, in which all markets of the economy (such as the markets for airline flights, oil and housing) are interconnected. This is a model of general equilibrium, in which the ratio of exchange between all possible goods is taken into account.

In what follows, we will first briefly consider Antoine Augustin Cournot (1801–77), as his work had a major impact on the mathematical model of Walras. We will then follow Walras's reasoning regarding simple acts of exchange, which is indeed very similar to Jevons's "mechanics of utility and self-interest". Finally, we will investigate his general equilibrium theory, which describes the economy as a (large) set of equations that are determined simultaneously. Since Walras's work, even more than that of Jevons, relies on extensive algebra, we will try to provide a general description of his reasoning without emphasizing all the technical details.

Cournot's *Researches*

We mentioned Cournot briefly in the previous chapter as his work occupies a prominent place in Jevons's list of mathematical-economic writings. He also had a profound influence on the development of Walras's general equilibrium theory.

Cournot's mathematical treatment of economics cannot really be labelled "marginalism", but he should be credited for defining and drawing the first demand function (Blaug 1962: 301). Cournot's *Researches into the Mathematical Principles of the Theory of Wealth* appeared in 1838, but it did not receive much attention at the time. Contrary to authors such as Gossen, Dupuit and Jevons, Cournot (1838: 10–11) argues that "utility, scarcity, and suitability to the needs and enjoyments of mankind" are not suitable foundations for a science, since they are variable and by nature indeterminate. There is "no fixed standard for the utility of things", since everybody makes different estimates. Value in exchange is a "fixed" and "definite" idea and should be used to define wealth. For instance, a bookseller may increase his wealth by destroying two-thirds of the editions of a certain book, as he may now be able to sell the remaining third at a significantly higher price. At first sight his wealth decreases (since some of his books are destroyed), but since the value in exchange of his remaining books has increased, in the end his wealth has also increased.

Wealth can therefore be defined in terms of value in exchange (or price). The demand for a certain good D should be seen as a function F of price p, or in mathematical symbols: $D = F(p)$. When the price goes down, the quantity demanded will increase. This mathematical relationship between p and D is expressed by the function F. This "law of demand" does depend on the utility of the good, on habits and customs, on wealth and on wealth distribution, but in general, demand will increase when a good gets cheaper, and demand will go down when a good becomes more expensive. In other words, demand (or quantity demanded) is a decreasing function of price. If this function is continuous, then small changes in price will lead to "sensibly proportional" small changes in quantity (Cournot 1838: 44–50). Cournot makes a direct connection between price and quantity demanded but does not consider the underlying theory of (marginal) utility that is so crucial for authors such as Gossen and Jevons.

Cournot's mathematical analysis is rigorous and strikingly modern to the contemporary reader, but we can summarize the essence of his arguments as follows. Cournot applies the notion of the demand function to the monopoly case, i.e. the situation when only one supplier provides a certain good. If this monopolist wants to sell more units, then he needs to lower his price. A lower price will attract additional customers, and existing customers may decide to buy more units. On the one hand, revenue will increase because more units are sold; but on the other hand, the price per unit goes down, which again decreases revenue. We also need to take the cost of production into account: the seller can only increase his profit if the additional (or marginal) revenue from selling another unit is higher than the additional (or marginal) cost incurred because of the additional production. Profit is equal to total revenue (which is price times quantity) minus total costs. Profit is therefore a multivariate function that depends on price, quantity (which is itself a function of price) and cost (which is itself a function of quantity). In order to maximize profits, we need to apply differential calculus. As all students of microeconomics know, profit maximization occurs where marginal revenue becomes equal to marginal cost. If marginal revenue exceeds marginal cost, then the monopolist wants to sell more; if marginal revenue is smaller than marginal cost, then the monopolist wants to sell less.

Cournot then considers a duopoly, i.e. competition between two firms, where each firm regards the quantity offered by the rival firm as constant. It turns out that the market price goes down when more and more firms are added to the competitive process. This model is currently known as Cournot quantity competition, and it occupies a prominent place in the field of industrial organization. The field studies the phenomenon of imperfect competition, which occurs when some firms have substantial market power (a situation that is often called an "oligopoly"). Many modern markets are dominated by only a few large firms (such as Ab Inbev and Heineken in the beer market), and therefore the analysis of imperfect competition is of the utmost importance. We will say more about imperfect competition and industrial organization in chapter 8.

Like most other authors of the nineteenth century, Walras mainly considers cases in which no such market power exists. This is now commonly called a market in which "perfect competition" occurs: no firm is sufficiently large or powerful to have a substantial impact on the market price. Although Walras does not follow in Cournot's footsteps when it comes to the analysis of monopoly, he does utilize his mathematical treatment of demand in functional form.

Wealth and value

Before we can consider Walras's treatment of demand, we need to investigate his notion of "wealth". Walras defines "social wealth" as all things, both material and immaterial, that are useful, on the one hand, and limited in quantity (and therefore scarce), on the other. Scarcity is an intrinsically mathematical concept, comparable to velocity in mechanics. We might describe objects being "slow" and "fast", but the natural scientist would refer to "lower" or "higher" velocity. In economics, "scarcity" and "abundance" are not opposed, but simply a matter of degree. Things that are unlimited in quantity, and therefore have a level of scarcity equal to zero, are not a part of social wealth. For instance, air is not scarce and therefore is not a part of social wealth. Social wealth is thus the collection of all useful things that have a level of scarcity greater than zero.

This definition of "social wealth" has three consequences. First of all, useful things that are limited in quantity are appropriable, which means that individuals can obtain them and thus become their owner. Second, they are valuable and exchangeable, so they can and will be traded on the market. Finally, they can be produced and multiplied by industry. Once appropriated, scarce things acquire value in the process of exchange. This exchange is carried out in the market, where value in exchange appears to be a natural phenomenon – for instance, we could observe that bananas cost €1.89 per kilogram. This exchange value could of course be altered by government intervention: the price of bananas could be fixed at €1.50, the stock could be destroyed or the trade in bananas could be outlawed altogether. However, if freedom prevails in the market, then the value of exchange will be determined by supply and demand, and therefore by scarcity.

Since values in exchange are magnitudes that are expressed in numbers, mathematics is required to study this phenomenon. The field of mathematics examines ideal types, such as perfect geometrical figures, that we do not find as such in reality. Pure economics deals with ideal types as well. Ideal markets and ideal prices only approximate real markets and real prices, but they are nevertheless useful for the study of real markets. In short, pure economics should be deductive ("rational"), which means that we can infer consequences from ideal types, rather than follow an inductive path ("experimental"), i.e. we can collect data in order to arrive at empirically established laws (Walras 1874: 65–72).[2]

---

2. The difference between deductive and inductive reasoning can be illustrated with a simple example. If we know for sure that all ravens are black, then we can bring forward the law "all ravens are black". The "raven" is here an ideal type, and the colour "black" is an essential feature of this ideal type. Before we see any particular raven, we already know that it will be black, as we know for sure that the law "all ravens are black" is true. An inductive approach takes the opposite route. I can observe a raven and notice that

Value in exchange is established in the market, where commodities, or things that are valuable and exchangeable, are traded. Value in exchange is therefore determined by competition. The purest form of competition can be found at the stock exchange, where investment products such as shares and bonds are bought and sold. Competition is also present in other markets (such as grain markets, shoe shops, or even the market in which the value of a doctor's consultations is determined), but compared with the stock exchange this competition is organized poorly.

Since pure economics follows a deductive approach, we need to suppose that the market is perfectly competitive. By examining competition in its purest form, we avoid investigating exchange under unusual conditions. An example would be studying the exchange of diamonds or unique paintings, which cannot lead us to generally applicable conclusions. For any price of a share or a bond that is traded at the stock exchange, an effective offer and an effective demand for the share or bond will be established. The word "effective" indicates that a budget is available: a poor person may demand shares or bonds, but he does not have the budget to actually buy them.

At a given price, some traders would want to buy the bond or share, whereas others would like to sell it. If the quantity demanded is equal to the quantity supplied, then the market is in equilibrium. In the case of disequilibrium, the price needs to change. A higher price will reduce effective demand and increase effective offer (i.e. effective supply); a lower price will have the opposite effect. The price will therefore change continuously until effective demand and effective offer are in equilibrium.

In the simplest case of exchange between two commodities, however, there is only a direct and immediate effect between price and effective demand (as the consumer can change his consumption pattern immediately), whereas the effect between price and effective offer is indirect and delayed (as it

---

it is black. Then I can observe a second and then a third raven, and again see that they are black. If I have seen 100 ravens and they are all black, then I can conclude that "all ravens are black". We have established a law following an inductive process. However, we can never be sure that we have actually seen all ravens. There may be a particular raven, hidden somewhere in the deepest rainforest, that has green or red feathers. It is therefore impossible to establish absolute and certain laws by following the route of induction. This is commonly known as the "problem of induction".

takes time to alter the process of production in order to produce more or less) (Walras 1874: 83–91). Walras constructs demand schedules, with price on the x-axis and quantity on the y-axis, which makes perfect sense since quantity is a function of price.[3]

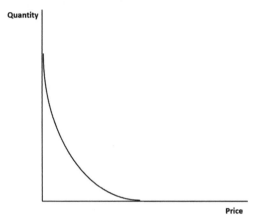

Figure 5.1 Walras's demand curve.
Source: Walras (1874: 94).

The market demand curve is established by summing up the individual demand curves of all traders that are active in the market. An individual demand curve may be discontinuous, which means that there may be large jumps in quantity demanded when the price changes.

For instance, I may decide that I will not buy bananas at all when they cost €1.90 or more per kilogram but that I would be willing to buy one kilogram at a price of €1.89. The market demand curve will, however, be continuous, because of the law of large numbers. When the price increases from €1.89 to €1.90, only a few people may decide not to purchase bananas. A small increase in price will then have a small effect on the total quantity demanded in the market. Figure 5.1 represents such a continuous market demand curve. As we can see in the graph, demand curves generally intersect the axes. The intersection on the quantity axis means that, even at a

---

3. Modern economists follow the convention to put price on the y-axis and quantity on the x-axis. Quantity can be seen as a function of price, but price can also be seen as a function of quantity, so this is indeed a matter of convention.

price of zero, individuals will not demand an infinite quantity. The intersection on the price axis implies that there is an extremely high price such that nobody can afford to purchase a single unit of the commodity. In the case of only two goods (without money, so that the goods are directly exchanged against each other), there are two demand curves and two supply curves, one for each of the goods, as functions of the price of these goods (expressed in terms of the quantity of the other good that must be given in exchange). Equilibrium prices are reached when effective demand and effective supply are equal for both commodities (Walras 1874: 92–106).

Walras's reasoning about the demand curve is similar to Cournot's thus far, but now he turns his attention to its underlying forces. He considers utility or want curves, which can be seen as the cause of exchange. He distinguishes between extensive and intensive utility. Extensive utility determines the quantity of a good demanded when its price is equal to zero: the good is freely available and its demand does not therefore depend on the other good. Intensive utility indicates the urgency of the desire for a certain good, and takes into account the sacrifice that needs to be made to acquire the good. This does take the other good into account, since in order to increase our quantity of the good, we need to decrease the quantity of the other (since we need to give the other good in exchange). The demand curves for the two commodities are then determined by each party's utility or want curves for these commodities, as well as the initial stock of these commodities owned by each party.

Walras then defines "effective utility" (or total utility) as "the sum total of wants satisfied by any given quantity consumed of a commodity", and "*rareté*" (or marginal utility) as "the intensity of the last want satisfied by any given quantity consumed of a commodity". All market participants will try to achieve a maximum satisfaction of wants, or a maximum total utility, by participating in exchange. If a market participant has a large stock of a certain good, then one unit of the stock will have a small marginal utility; he would be willing to exchange it for a good of which he has only a small stock, since one unit of that small stock will have a high marginal utility. But by giving up a unit of the large stock, the marginal utility of that good will increase, whereas the marginal utility of the good that he receives in exchange will decrease, since his stock of that good increases. In equilibrium, the ratio of *raretés* (or marginal utilities) will be equal to the relative price (which is the ratio between the values of exchange);

otherwise the participants will find it beneficial to continue their exchange (Walras 1874: 115–31). This reasoning is basically equivalent to Jevons's discussion of two trading bodies exchanging beef and corn, which we discussed in the previous chapter.[4]

Rareté (or marginal utility) is an *absolute* phenomenon, as it depends on the utility of a commodity and on the quantity of that commodity possessed by the holder. At the same time, *rareté* (or marginal utility) is a personal or *subjective* phenomenon, since it differs from person to person. Value in exchange, on the other hand, is a *relative* phenomenon, as values in exchange (or prices) are proportional (and thus relative) to the *raretés* or marginal utilities. But given that these prices (or relative values in exchange) prevail in the entire market (as there can only be one price in the market), value in exchange is also a real or *objective* phenomenon.[5]

Now suppose that, starting from an equilibrium situation, for some reason an increase in utility occurs for one of the two goods (we will call this one good A) and for one of the two market participants. At the prevailing relative market price, this person will no longer derive maximum satisfaction. He or she would find it beneficial to demand more of this good (good A) with higher utility, by offering more of the other good (which we will call good B) in exchange. The demand for good A will therefore increase, whereas the demand for good B (which is equivalent to the supply of good A, since it is given in exchange for good B) will remain unchanged, as no change in utility has occurred for the other market participant. The relative market price for good A must therefore increase, implying that the other market participant will also no longer derive maximum satisfaction. The latter will now also be willing to participate in the market exchange, by offering some of good A in exchange for some of good B. A new equilibrium will be established, with a

---

4. Walras (1874: 204–6) indicates that Jevons managed to derive the equations of exchange. However, he also notes two differences. Where Walras uses prices, defined as the reciprocals of the ratios of the quantities of the commodities exchanged, Jevons uses ratios of exchange, defined as the direct ratios of the quantities of the commodities exchanged. Furthermore, Jevons's analysis is limited to the special case when only two parties are involved in the act of exchange. The development of general equilibrium theory requires that prices, and not quantities exchanged, should be considered to be the unknowns.

5. Note that this is a simple model with only two goods, and that there is no good that could function as "numéraire" or money good. Therefore, a market price in this simple model is always a relative price, as it expresses how much a unit of one good is worth in terms of units of the other good.

higher relative price for good A and a lower relative price for good B. This reasoning shows that *rareté*, or marginal utility, is actually the cause of value in exchange (Walras 1874: 143–9).

We may illustrate this abstract reasoning with a simple example. Consider Paul and Mary, two consumers who can exchange apples for bananas (and bananas for apples). One apple can be exchanged for one banana, which corresponds to the relative valuations of both Paul and Mary. The condition of maximum satisfaction is therefore fulfilled, so that exchange will not increase the utility for either Paul or Mary. Assume that Paul is suffering from a rare disease and that new scientific research reveals that apples may actually cure his illness. Paul's extensive utility will increase, since he will now consume more apples if they are freely available. But his intensive utility will also increase, as he will now be willing to exchange more bananas for apples. Suppose that he wants to exchange two bananas for one apple. Mary would be willing to engage in this exchange, as she still values apples and bananas equally and she could now get two bananas for one apple. As we saw before, every act of exchange changes the relative valuations, as the available quantity of the goods for both consumers will change. Exchange will go on until a new condition of maximum satisfaction is reached. It is clear that Paul will hold more apples and fewer bananas than before, that Mary will hold fewer apples and more bananas, and that the relative price of apples (in terms of bananas) will have increased whereas the relative price of bananas (in terms of apples) will be lower.

General equilibrium theory: exchange

The above reasoning is still very similar to Jevons's theory of exchange. However, in part III of EPE, Walras extends his model to deal with exchange in more than two commodities. If there are m goods, then the effective demand for every good will depend on the relative prices of all the other goods. This is clear for related goods, as in the case of airline flights and oil that we mentioned before. But it must also be the case for all goods that are available. If the price of bread increases, and I nevertheless want to consume the same amount of bread as before, then I will have less income left to be spent on all other goods. If the good takes up a large share of my budget, as in the case of housing, then my demand for all other goods may be affected negatively in a strong way. The quantity demanded for every good is a function not only of its own price, but also of the prices of all the other available goods.

Every good can be exchanged for any of the other goods. For each of the m goods in our economy, we therefore have $(m - 1)$ equations of effective demand, or $m(m - 1)$ equations of effective demand in total. Furthermore, for each of the m goods we can also establish $(m - 1)$ equations of exchange, which express equality between effective demand and effective offer. For each of the m goods we therefore have $(m - 1)$ equations of exchange, which will give us $m(m - 1)$ equations in total (since there are m goods). This would give us a total of $2m(m - 1)$ equations, which corresponds to the amount of unknowns: the $m(m - 1)$ prices for the goods expressed in terms of all the other goods, plus the $m(m - 1)$ total quantities for each of the goods exchanged for each of the other goods. For three goods, we would therefore have six equations of effective demand and six equations of exchange, but also six prices for the three goods, each expressed in terms of the other two, and six quantities of the three goods exchanged for one another. If we have ten goods, then we will have a total of no less than 180 equations and unknowns, and this number increases exponentially when more goods are added to the model. The number of equations is therefore the same as the number of unknowns, which implies that the algebraic system can be solved.

At least in theory, this reasoning would allow us to determine the equilibrium prices for all goods available in a certain market, and we are no longer restricted to simple cases with only two goods and two consumers. But it is also true that the number of equations and unknowns increases dramatically when more goods are added to the model. Fortunately, modern economists can use computers and software for this purpose.

Walras's theory provides a model of general equilibrium in which equilibrium must be attained in all markets of the economy: "We do not have perfect or general market equilibrium unless the price of one of any two commodities in terms of the other is equal to the ratio of the prices of these two commodities in terms of any third commodity" (Walras 1874: 157). If one market is not in equilibrium, than at least one other market must also not be in equilibrium. And if there are m markets, and $(m - 1)$ markets are in equilibrium, then the remaining market must also be in equilibrium.

The movement of the economy towards general equilibrium is called "*tâtonnement*" or "groping": a process of trial and error in which a multitude of prices is "tried out" until a set of equilibrium prices is finally reached for which all markets in the economy are in equilibrium.

So far Walras has only considered goods that are exchanged for other goods, but exchange usually takes place using a form of money. We may define one good as the money good or numéraire, such as gold, and we can then express the price of any good in terms of this numéraire. Adding money to the system does not fundamentally alter the model, as we simply add another good that functions as the numéraire. If the utility of a certain good increases, everything else remaining equal, then the price of that good in terms of the numéraire will increase. More gold will be required to purchase the good.

This is often seen as an instance of the "law of supply and demand": when the demand for a certain good goes up, the price for that good will increase. However, this "law of supply and demand" is presented as a sort of empirical observation (see, for example, Cournot), and there is no theory that really explains why increased demand leads to a higher price. This formulation fails to define effective demand (i.e. a demand that actually results in a purchase, given the budget of the consumer), and does not show the relationship between *rareté* (or marginal utility) and price (Walras 1874: 173–81). The point is that the demand increased because the utility of the good increased – the simple reference to the (apparently straightforward) "law of supply and demand" conceals the important relationship between utility and price. Marginal utility is therefore indispensable if we want to describe the fundamental law of supply and demand in a meaningful way. Any theory of exchange requires the notion of "marginal utility".

General equilibrium theory: production

Of course, the economy consists of more than simply exchange. Goods and commodities are not only exchanged, they are also products resulting from the combination of productive factors such as labour, land and capital. In order to cope with production, Walras needs to extend his model. He does this by modelling production as a form of exchange: namely, the exchange of services derived from these productive factors. Walras first distinguishes between capital and income. Capital – also called fixed capital – is that part of social wealth that can be used more than once, such as buildings and machines. Income – also called circulating capital – is that part of social wealth that can be used only once, such as food products and raw materials. Some parts of social wealth could be capital but also income: trees are capital when they bear fruit, but they become income when they are chopped down for lumber. Capital gives rise to income through services, which are defined as activities consisting of the use of capital. Consumer services – such as the shelter given by a house or a consultation undertaken by a doctor – are consumed in their original form. Productive services are transformed by agriculture, industry or commerce into products: the fertility of the soil, the labour of the workman, and the use of machines and tools provide products. Social wealth then consists of four categories, three of capital and one of income:

- land, yielding land-income or land-services or "*rentes*";
- persons, yielding personal incomes or services of persons, called "labour";
- capital proper, yielding capital-income or capital-services or "profits"; and finally
- income, consisting of consumers' goods and raw materials (Walras 1874: 211–17).

The three categories of capital (land, persons and capital proper) are held by three groups of individuals: landowners, workers and capitalists. In addition, the entrepreneur is the person who leases land, hires labour and borrows capital, in order to combine these productive services in agriculture, industry or commerce. Of course, one and the same individual can combine two or more of these functions, just as when the entrepreneur is also the owner of the land or the capital, or works in his own business.

Walras then distinguishes between the services market and the products market. In the services market, the entrepreneur buys productive services from landowners, workers and capitalists by paying them rent, wages and interest, respectively (in terms of the numéraire). In the products market, the entrepreneur sells his or her products to these three groups of owners of productive services, again in terms of the numéraire. Exchange in the services market operates in basically the same way as exchange in the products market.[6] If the selling price of a product exceeds the cost of the services used as inputs, then more entrepreneurs will be attracted into this branch of production, which will increase the supply of that product and therefore lower its price. If the selling price turns out to be lower than the production cost, the opposite will happen. In equilibrium, therefore, the product price will be equal to the input cost and entrepreneurs will make zero profit (Walras 1874: 222–6).

It is then possible to formulate a set of equations describing the products as well as the services market, both operating under free competition. The products will sell if three conditions are satisfied: maximum satisfaction of wants, each product and service has a uniform price (the law of one price), and general equilibrium is established. Equilibrium will be established if effective demand and supply are equal for all products and services and the selling price of all products is equal to the cost of the services used as inputs (Walras 1874: 243–54). It is beyond the scope of this book to discuss in detail Walras's theory of capital formation and capitalization, which is discussed in Part V of EPE, but we can state that the same principles that were discussed above will also apply here.[7]

We can conclude that Walras's general equilibrium approach goes beyond Jevons's utilitarian mechanics. Whereas Jevons's reasoning about exchange is restricted to simple cases, with two trading bodies and two goods, Walras extends marginalism to general equilibrium theory, which depicts the entire economy as a set of mathematical equations that are interrelated. The price of every good has an impact on the price of every other good, and therefore on all quantities demanded. The functional relationship between prices and

---

6. Walras (1874: 242) notes two differences that make the process of groping (*"tâtonnement"*) towards equilibrium more complicated in production than it is with the exchange of goods. Whereas in product exchange the total quantity of the commodities does not change when new prices are established, in production the quantities of products must be revised. Furthermore, production takes time, whereas exchange can take place immediately.

7. Demand for capital goods comes from individuals who have an excess of income over consumption; supply of these capital goods comes from individuals with income lower than consumption. Under free competition, the principles of maximum effective utility and uniformity of price will lead to capital formation best suited to generate the greatest possible satisfaction of wants, and this will yield capital prices sufficient to cover the costs of depreciation and insurance of capital goods (Walras 1874: 305–6).

quantities demanded is explained by the theory of marginal utility. Walras integrated production into his model by regarding production as a form of exchange: namely, the exchange of services that are provided by the different factors of production. In doing so, he treated all factors of production equally, as the prices of their services are all to be explained by marginalist principles.

Many economists, especially in France and Italy, have extended general equilibrium theory, which is still a part of any modern course in intermediate general equilibrium theory. An important issue in this literature concerns the conditions that need to be fulfilled in order to achieve general equilibrium, as well as the stability of this general equilibrium. Walras would simply count the equations and unknowns, and conclude that the system of equations can be solved if the number of equations is equal to the number of unknowns. Modern microeconomics has moved far beyond this point and has developed into a very technical branch of economics that is barely accessible to outsiders.[8] What now remains is an investigation of Carl Menger's contribution to the marginal revolution, which differs in many respects from the strictly mathematical approaches of Jevons and Walras.

---

8. A milestone in this development is the paper "Existence of an equilibrium for a competitive economy" by Kenneth Arrow and Gerard Debreu, which was published in 1954. It is a very technical paper that investigates which conditions need to be fulfilled in order to arrive at a general equilibrium in an economy that is perfectly competitive. To put it simply, we can say that all indifference curves (which we will meet in chapter 8), which represent the preferences of the consumers, must be strictly convex, i.e. they must have the conventional shape that students of microeconomics know from their textbooks.

6

Carl Menger, Friedrich von Wieser and the Austrian approach

Menger is generally seen as the founder of the Austrian school of economics, which emerged in the second half of the nineteenth century. Most of
the present adherents of this school are, however, to be found in the United
States.

The Austrian school is a "non-mainstream" or "heterodox" approach in
economic theory that differs fundamentally from the mainstream approach
of economics.[1] The mainstream approach to economics developed from
the writings of authors such as Jevons and Walras. Both Jevons and Walras
approach the economy from a static point of view, which means that they
are interested in the equilibrium conditions that prevail after all processes
of exchange have ceased. According to Jevons, the process of exchange of
two goods between two trading bodies will cease as soon as the ratio of
exchange becomes equal to the relative valuations of the goods, for both
trading bodies. According to Walras, a general equilibrium is achieved
when the equilibrium prices of all goods and services are established in
such a way that no further gains in exchange are possible. These equilibrium
conditions are themselves the subject for examination, rather than the more
complicated dynamical processes that lead to the equilibrium.

The Austrian school took a different route. In their view, the world is in
a constant state of flux, and there is no state of equilibrium at any point.
Competition should be regarded as an ongoing process, in which one competitor tries to outsmart the others by providing better products, at a lower

---

1. "Until 1960 *Austrian economics* was considered part of the mainstream; but as neoclassical economics faded and mainstream economics opted for formal model building,
the Austrians reemerged as dissenters" (Landreth & Colander 2002: 494).

price, and by applying a wide variety of marketing tactics. Whereas Jevons and Walras use marginalism as a principle to determine equilibrium conditions, Menger investigates the role of marginalism within the process of decision-making. Furthermore, the Austrian approach can be characterized as "subjective" and "individualistic": all economic actions must be explained by the rational behaviour of an individual agent, who approaches the world from his/her own subjective point of view. These points of view may differ substantially between individuals, and consequently Austrian economists do not typically presuppose perfect information (which implies the unrealistic assumption that everybody knows everything). On the contrary, the Austrian school emphasizes that mistakes are possible in the process of decision-making but also that learning (from mistakes) plays an important role. This "process-oriented" and "subjective" approach means that Menger and his followers provide a unique perspective on marginalism that differs substantially from the works of both Jevons and Walras. Austrian economic theory can also be seen as the logic of economic decision-making. Since Menger does not focus on equilibrium conditions, he has little use for mathematics and calculus. In what follows we first examine Menger's writings and then those of Friedrich von Wieser (1851–1926), who provides a more elaborate Austrian treatment of marginalist theory.

Menger on economic goods of a lower and higher order

Menger starts his analysis with a definition of a good (*"Gut"*). A thing can be a "good" if four conditions are fulfilled:

1. there must be a particular human desire or need (*"Bedürfniss"*);
2. a causal relationship exists, i.e. the thing can contribute to fulfilling this human desire;
3. humans need to recognize this causal relationship; and
4. the thing must be available, so that the desire can actually be satisfied.

For instance, consider the basic need for food. There is a causal relationship when insects are eaten to satiate the desire for food, but the potential for using insects as human food has only recently become a widely recognized proposition. Fortunately, insects are widely available, so they may become a major food product of the future.

A thing may also lose its capacity to be a good if either the particular human desire for it, or the causal relationship or knowledge of it, or the availability of the thing were to disappear. Goods can be imaginary ("*einge-bildet*") if humans mistakenly believe that a thing can satisfy a need, such as medication that does not work.

There are basically two categories of goods: material objects ("*Sachgüter*") and useful human actions ("*nützliche menschliche Handlungen*"). Regarding the latter, even an omission ("*Unterlassung*") of human action can be a good: for instance, it would be a good for a doctor practising in a small village if the other doctor in the village stopped practising, so that she can then achieve a monopoly position (allowing her to charge higher prices). Goods can also be subdivided into categories according to their position in the causal relationship. For instance, bread can be directly consumed to fulfil a human desire (hunger), whereas flour's use is indirectly linked, because it is used to produce the bread. The bread can be seen as a good of the first order, flour as a good of the second order, wheat and corn mills (which are used to produce the flour) are goods of the third order, and so forth.

Menger emphasizes that being a good is not an intrinsic characteristic of anything, since its role as a good is determined by its potential to fulfil human needs and by its position in the causal relationship (Menger 1871: 1–10). The goods of a higher order (second, third and so on) may lose their status as goods if required complementary goods are no longer available. For instance, the American Civil War led to a shortage of cotton in Europe, which in turn made the labour of textile workers in Europe superfluous, and this labour therefore lost its status as a "good". Furthermore, whether a thing is a good of a higher order or not depends on the good of a lower order: if people suddenly stopped smoking and no longer consumed tobacco (a good of the first order), then the tobacco seeds and plants, certain tools and bits of land, and the labour of workers in the tobacco industry (goods of higher orders) would lose their status as goods, unless they could be repurposed.

Menger emphasizes that it takes time to transform goods of a higher order into goods of a lower order, and that there is uncertainty about the quantity and quality of the final product, and that mistakes are therefore possible (Menger 1871: 11–26). This may all seem trivial, but it is a remarkable distinction between his writings and those of Jevons and Walras, who did not elaborate on the role of time and presupposed "perfect information" as a prerequisite for a perfectly competitive market. Menger repeats Adam Smith's discussion of the division of labour, which contributes to the increasing wealth of nations, but adds that scientific progress, i.e. the growth of the understanding of causal processes, is also very important. This understanding allows the production of goods of a higher order, which lengthens the production process and allows humans to produce goods that are not meant for immediate consumption (such as the accumulation of winter stock during the summer) (Menger 1871: 26–35).

Economic goods are those goods for which the desire is greater than the available quantity. Only these economic goods are relevant for economic processes. If a river produces more water than is required to fulfil all the needs of a certain community, then the river would be a non-economic good. There is no incentive for the inhabitants to develop goods of a higher order to increase the water supply (Menger 1871: 51–70). As a result, only economic goods have value: for non-economic goods, there is always a partial quantity left over.

If a forest dweller is surrounded by thousands of trees but only requires 20 per year to fulfil his desire for wood, then the trees would be non-economic goods and they would have no value. If a fire were to destroy half of the forest, then the inhabitant's ability to fulfil his desire for wood would be unaffected. If, on the other hand, there were only 10 fruit-bearing trees available in the forest, and the amount of available fruit was only just sufficient to satisfy his desire for fruit, then the loss of just one of these fruit trees would immediately affect his ability to fulfil all his needs for fruit. Some of his need would remain unsatisfied. This implies that the fruit trees are economic goods and therefore have value for the forest dweller.

Some economists have suggested that non-economic goods can also have a use value, but Menger argues that this confuses "usefulness" with "value in use". The non-fruit-bearing trees are certainly useful for the inhabitant of the forest, since they provide him with wood, but these trees are so abundant that they have no value in use: a reduction in the number of trees would not impede the inhabitant's ability to completely fulfil all his desire for wood. These trees could only become economic goods, and therefore acquire value (in use), if almost the entire forest were destroyed, or if the population of the forest increased substantially. Being valuable is therefore not an intrinsic characteristic of a thing, but it is intrinsically subjective as it is relative to the possible fulfilment of human desires (which may be imaginary, as we saw above). Moreover, a thing can only be an economic good (and therefore acquire value) if it is not available in unlimited quantity (relative to the desires that need to be fulfilled) (Menger 1871: 77–86).

Menger's "Scala" and the theory of value

Given that "value" is something variable, Menger examines the causes of this variability. He distinguishes between the "subjective moment" and the "objective moment". The subjective moment addresses the fact that the fulfilment of different desires may have different meanings. In order of importance, the desire to preserve life is the greatest; this is followed by the preservation of good health; and only then follow forms of enjoyment that we consider to be luxuries. For example, only a very small portion of our food consumption is strictly necessary for the preservation of our lives. A further portion is required to maintain our good health. Another portion can then be seen as a luxury. As a rule we all consume more food than is strictly required, simply because we enjoy eating.

Without using its terminology, Menger expresses the law of diminishing marginal utility (Gossen's first law): the first mouthfuls of a meal provide more enjoyment than those that follow, and so on, because the earlier mouthfuls fulfil more important desires than the later ones. Menger illustrates his argument with his "Scala" (Figure 6.1). The Roman numerals (at the top of every column) indicate different desires, such as (for example) the desire to consume food (I) and the desire to enjoy tobacco (V). Every column contains numbers that indicate the importance of the fulfilled desires. The first number in column I is a 10, which means that here the desire for food is concerned with the preservation of life. By increasing our food consumption we can satisfy less important desires: first the preservation of good health, and thereafter we consume food for luxury purposes. As we move down scale I, the allocated score therefore decreases. Clearly, the enjoyment of tobacco is not concerned with the preservation of life or health (quite the opposite), and the first score in column V is therefore only a 6. Only when our most important desires to consume food are fulfilled (when we have reached number 6 in column I) will the desire to enjoy tobacco make an appearance. In modern terminology, we would say that continued food consumption decreases the marginal utility of food to below 6, at which point it will become more enjoyable to consume tobacco (column V) rather than to continue eating food.

I	II	III	IV	V	VI	VII	VIII	IX	X
10	9	8	7	6	5	4	3	2	1
9	8	7	6	5	4	3	2	1	0
8	7	6	5	4	3	2	1	0	
7	6	5	4	3	2	1	0		
6	5	4	3	2	1	0			
5	4	3	2	1	0				
4	3	2	1	0					
3	2	1	0						
2	1	0							
1	0								
0									

Figure 6.1 Menger's Scala.
Source: Menger (1871: 93).

The Scala suggests that Menger followed a "cardinal" approach to utility, meaning that "utility" can be expressed using a number. However, Menger makes no calculations, and the numbers are merely used to rank different degrees of utility satisfaction rather than to provide quantitative measures of utility as such. He follows an "ordinal" approach to utility, which enables different desires to be ranked though not (necessarily) measured exactly or expressed in a precise quantitative form (Menger 1871: 87–95).[2]

The "objective moment" addresses the fact that one and the same good may fulfil different kinds of desires, which is important if the available quantity of the good is limited. For instance, if an individual requires 20 units of water to preserve his life, another 40 units to preserve his health and wealth, and yet another 40 units for luxury purposes (e.g. watering his flower garden), then the water will have no value for him as long as more than 100 units are available. Reducing the water supply by one unit will not

---

2. For more about Menger (and Jevons and Walras) and cardinal utility, see Moscati (2013).

change his ability to fulfil all his desires. If only 90 units are available, he would have to give up satisfying some of his luxury desires: the water would then have some value for him. If only 40 units were available, he would have to give up satisfying his luxury desires entirely and he would be unable to preserve his health and wealth in full: in this case, the value of the water would increase. If the supply of water were to be reduced to only 20 units, every unit would be required to maintain his life and water would therefore be given a score of 10 according to the Scala.

This reasoning can also be applied in a social setting: for instance, on a sailing ship that carries a limited amount of food (a dry biscuit or "hardtack" (*"Zwieback"*)) on board. If everybody on board requires 10 pounds of hardtack to survive, and if everybody has exactly 10 pounds at his disposal, then nobody would be willing to exchange a pound of hardtack for something else – not even for gold. But even if everybody were given 15 pounds of hardtack, one pound would be extremely valuable, because consuming a few pounds more than is strictly necessary for the preservation of life would clearly be beneficial for the health and well-being of an individual. The food would only have no value if there were such an abundant supply that everybody could take as much as he wanted. In every situation, the passengers would be the same and their desires would also be the same. The only difference is the quantity of food available on the ship. It follows that the value of a pound of hardtack is determined by the least important (*"die wenigst wichtigen"*) desires that could be satisfied by that pound of hardtack.

This approach also resolves Adam Smith's water–diamond paradox: water is necessary for the preservation of life (it is very useful) but it is so abundant that reducing the water supply by one unit would not impede the ability of individuals to fulfil all their desires (it therefore has a low value); diamonds, on the other hand, are not very useful at all, but the supply of them is so limited that even the satisfaction of the least important desires still has a relatively high importance (Menger 1871: 113–4). In other words, the scale that represents the desire for water would start with a 10 (necessary for the preservation of life), but since water is so abundant we move down quickly to 0. The scale that represents the desire for diamonds would start with a much lower number (2 or 1, say, in column IX or X), but since the supply is so limited we would never reach the bottom of the scale. This relationship would be reversed in the desert, where nobody would be able to buy water in exchange for diamonds.[3]

Menger's theory of value is therefore centred around subjective valuation on the one hand and available supply on the other. Other approaches, such as the cost or labour theory of value, are in his opinion mistaken. The comparison between the value of a product and the value of the means of production (labour, land, capital) required to generate that product is only retrospective, i.e. it tells us whether the productive activity in the past was economically effective or not (Menger 1871: 120). Menger also emphasizes that individuals tend to make mistakes in their valuations: sometimes in the "subjective moment" but more often in the "objective moment" (Menger 1871: 122).

But then what determines the value of the means of production, such as labour, land and capital? Clearly, these are goods of a higher order that are used to produce consumption goods, or goods of a lower order. The value of goods of a higher order does not determine the value of goods of a lower order – there is not even necessarily a connection between them. Means of production are used to generate products in the future, and it is therefore the *expected* value of future products that determines the present value of the means of production. If the value of a product increases today, then the value of the present means of production does not necessarily change. Only

---

3. Menger (1871: 213–24) elaborates on value in use and value in exchange in a short chapter. Value in use refers to the direct ability of a good to satisfy a certain need. Value in exchange is the indirect ability, through exchange, to satisfy a need. Typically, an individual would want to exchange a good for another if its value in use were less than its value in exchange. Menger provides several examples to indicate that the relationship between value in use and value in exchange is not fixed. For a smoker, a certain quantity of tobacco will have a greater value in use than it has value in exchange, but if he gives up smoking, this relationship will be reversed and he will want to sell his remaining stock of tobacco. For a rich person, a slightly worn piece of clothing, whose value in use initially exceeded its value in exchange, may lose all its value in use while still maintaining a rather high value in exchange (in which case he wants to sell it). The most important factor in the relationship between value in use and value in exchange is the available quantity of the good: following a harvest, the value in exchange of corn will exceed the value in use for the farmer, and therefore he would like to sell some of his corn. By selling the corn, the farmer decreases his remaining quantity of corn (and therefore increases its value in use), and he will continue to sell corn until its value in use becomes larger than its value in exchange.

an increase in the expected value of future products will increase the value of present means of production (Menger 1871: 123–6).

Menger then turns his attention to the production of these future products. Individuals will first and foremost devote attention to the production of goods of a lower order, to be consumed in the present. Only when the present is secure will the future receive attention. As soon as individuals transform goods of a lower order, such as seeds for immediate consumption or labour used in hunting, into goods of a higher order, such as seeds and labour used in agriculture, capital will emerge. The goods of a higher order, required for the generation of goods of a lower order in the future, will become capital. Moreover, goods that were initially non-economic, such as land or materials, may now become economic goods. Production takes time, which implies that the goods of a higher order will be tied to the production process for a shorter or longer period. In other words, the capital needs to remain invested for a certain amount of time and cannot be used for other purposes. The expected value of a future good of a lower order must therefore also include remuneration for the use of capital, and also for the activity of the entrepreneur (*"Unternehmer"*) who sets up the production process in the first place (Menger 1871: 127–38).

It also needs to be remembered that the goods of a higher order can be used in different amounts: for instance, more or less manure, or more or less manual labour, may be applied to a piece of land. The value of a certain quantity of a good of a higher order (e.g. manual labour) is therefore the difference between the satisfaction of needs achieved when this quantity is available and when it is not, given the availability of the other complementary goods (e.g. manure, tools). Suppose that the absence of a particular labourer in a shoe factory means that 20 fewer pairs of shoes are made. The value of that labour is then equal to the needs that could have been satisfied had these 20 pairs of shoes been produced. This reasoning is applicable to all goods of a higher order, including land and labour. The value of a piece of land (when combined with all complementary goods required for its cultivation, including remuneration for the use of capital and for the activity of the entrepreneur) is determined by the expected future value of the goods of a lower order resulting from the process of cultivation. Contrary to Ricardo, Menger therefore concludes that even land of the lowest quality would generate rent, as it contributes to the production of goods of a lower order. There is also no reason why wages – the remuneration for labour – should necessarily be at subsistence level. Wages (the price of labour) are determined by the value of the satisfaction of the needs that would not occur if we did not utilize this labour (Menger 1871: 138–52).

Menger on exchange

The division of labour implies that individuals satisfy consumption desires not only by producing goods themselves but also by trading with other individuals. The emergence of trade can therefore be explained by the desire of individuals to satisfy all their needs, not by a natural desire for trade in itself. An individual will not engage in trade unless they might benefit from it. If a farmer has more corn than he requires, then he would be willing to trade with a wine producer who has more wine than he requires. In this case, the superfluous corn has no value for the farmer, and the superfluous wine has no value for the wine producer. But even if these goods were to have some value for both parties, trade would be beneficial if three conditions were fulfilled.

1. If both parties own quantities of goods that have less value for them than they would have for the trading partner.
2. If both parties recognize that this is the case.
3. It they have the power to actually complete the trade.

Menger illustrates the process of trade with a numerical example in which farmers exchange horses for cows. For any farmer, the first horse (or cow) will be more valuable than the second horse (or cow), given that the first animal satisfies the most important needs of the farmer. The second horse (or cow) will be more valuable than the third, and so on. It will therefore be beneficial for both parties to trade as long as an additional cow is more valuable to the first farmer than the last horse in his possession, and at the same time the second farmer would find an additional horse more valuable than the last cow in his possession (Menger 1871: 153–71).

Trade implies that a market price is established. Given the subjective character of value, this price cannot be seen as something that objectively equalizes certain quantities of goods: a farmer will exchange a horse for a cow because the cow is more valuable to him than the horse, whereas the opposite must be the case for his trading partner. There is no objective equivalence between the horse and the cow, and therefore the price does not equalize the horse and the cow.

Suppose that an individual (A) regarded 100 units of his corn as being equivalent to 40 units of wine. He would only be willing to engage in trade if he could get 40 units of wine for less than 100 units of corn. He would therefore need to find another individual (B) who would be willing to give up 40 units of his wine for less than 100 units of corn: 80, say. In this situation there will be two boundaries: the price of 40 units of wine should less than 100, otherwise A would not be willing to trade; and it should be more than 80, otherwise B would not be interested in trading. The price for 40 units of wine will therefore be between 80 and 100 units of corn. The final market price will tend to become the average of the two limits (90 in this case), but it will basically be determined by haggling (*"feilschen"*) (Menger 1871: 172–9). Menger does not therefore establish a precise market price, given that the bargaining ability of the market participants needs to be taken into account.

Friedrich von Wieser's natural value

It is clear that Menger's reasoning is a form of marginalism, as he argues that the value of a product is determined by the conditions prevailing at the margin. The value of a good is determined by the least important desires that could not be fulfilled in the absence of the good. However, it can also be argued that the concept of "marginal utility" is not particularly central to Menger's economic theory (see chapter 1).

Other Austrian economists followed in Menger's footsteps. Probably the most elaborate Austrian treatment of "marginalism" can be found in Wieser's *Natural Value*, which was published in 1889. Wieser knows his precursors well and extensively cites authors such as Gossen, Jevons, Walras and Menger. His reasoning is in line with the work of these earlier authors, but his Austrian perspective offers different interpretations: regarding Gossen's second law, for instance (which we discussed in chapters 3 and 4). This law states that, when consumers must spread their income over many different branches of expenditure, the same degree of satisfaction – or the same marginal utility – must be reached for every branch. Wieser disagrees with this statement. Wieser takes money, which can be used to satisfy a large number of different desires, to illustrate his point. If the budget of a household increases, then typically the expenditure on only a few branches is increased, while the expenditure on others remains the same. The point is that every want has a "peculiar satiation scale" and that measuring the different wants against each other is not that simple:

> The principle for the economic employment of goods of manifold usefulness is not, then, that we must, in every employment, obtain the same lowest possible marginal utility, but that in all employment as low a marginal utility be reached as is possible without necessitating the loss, in some other employment, of a higher utility.
> (Wieser 1889: 15)

Modern economists would refer to this principle by using the concept of "opportunity costs". If I spend my budget on a wide range of different goods (shelter, food, clothing, etc.), then it does not follow that the last cent I spent on each of these "branches of expenditure" provides me with equal enjoyment. It is the total enjoyment derived from the whole budget that matters. It is not the marginal utility derived from spending an additional cent on shelter that matters: it is the marginal utility lost from not spending the additional cent on food, clothing and so on. This principle will become very important when we consider the optimal allocation of different means of production, as we will see below.

Wieser's reasoning is similar to Menger's, but his arguments are couched in terms of "marginal utility". It was actually Wieser who coined the term itself (*Grenznutzen* in German). The value of a stock of identical goods is determined by the marginal utility of the good. Suppose that we set up a scale of utility for bread: the first piece of bread is necessary for survival; the second piece is not that important, provided that we have the first piece. If our stock consists of only one piece, then this one piece (and therefore the stock) is extremely valuable, and we do not want to exchange it. If our stock consists of two pieces, then we could exchange one piece without endangering our life. The value of a piece of bread is therefore lower when we have two pieces than it is in the situation when we have only one piece. And since the two pieces of bread are identical, the value of the first piece is identical to the value of the second, and the value of the total stock (the two pieces of bread) is equal to twice the value of the piece of bread (which could be either of the two pieces) that we would be willing to exchange. The value of a piece of bread is therefore determined by the marginal utility of the bread: the utility that we would lose by giving up one piece. This also implies that the value of the stock (of identical pieces) as a whole is equal to the number of pieces in the stock multiplied by the marginal utility of one piece. We have seen above that when the supply increases, the marginal utility decreases (Gossen's first law). This explains why a small harvest may be more valuable than a large harvest: we have fewer goods in the first case, but the marginal utility of every good may be so large that the total value of the small harvest exceeds the total value of the large harvest, since in the latter case the marginal utility of every good will be much lower. If the supply of a good is so extensive that it becomes free, then the marginal utility falls to zero. In this case, the value of the stock would become zero, and nobody would bother to accumulate a stock of a free good.

Marginal value is therefore a combination of two elements: a positive one and a negative one. An additional good will increase value, since it will increase my enjoyment in the use of it. This positive effect is, however, accompanied by a negative effect, since a larger supply of any good will decrease its marginal utility. An additional piece of bread will, on the one hand, increase the value of my stock of bread, simply because I now have more bread available for use. On the other hand, by having more bread we will move down on the scale of utility, since the additional unit of bread will provide us with less additional utility than the units that we added earlier. But since all units of bread are identical, the marginal utility for all units of bread will go down. The additional unit of bread adds its marginal utility to the value of the stock (a positive effect), but it also deducts from the marginal utility of the earlier units of bread, and it therefore decreases the value of the stock (a negative effect). The value of a stock is zero if the stock consists of zero units; the value of the stock will increase when we add more units to the stock, until the negative effect becomes larger than the positive effect; and when the stock becomes so abundant that the good becomes free, the value of the stock will become zero again (Wieser 1889: 24–32).

Price formation

Wieser then considers price formation in a market. Suppose that a seller brings a fixed stock of goods to the market, and that he is confronted with a group of buyers that are ranked according to their willingness to buy the good, which is in turn determined by their desire for that good and by their wealth. The maximum that anybody would be willing to pay is determined by two magnitudes: (a) the value in use of the good and (b) the exchange value of the sum of money that would have to be paid. Let us further assume that every buyer only wants to buy one good. If there were only one good on offer, then the richest buyer would acquire it at a very high price. If there were two goods, then the second good would have to be sold to the second buyer at a lower price, since the second buyer is ranked lower than the first in terms of willingness to buy. But in that case, the first buyer would no longer need to pay the very high price that prevailed when only one good was available; the market price will therefore go down. When more goods are available and more buyers (with an ever-decreasing willingness to buy) enter the market, the market price will decrease. Eventually, the market price will be determined by the willingness to buy of the "marginal buyer", or the last buyer to participate in the market process.

This reasoning also holds when buyers would consider buying more than one unit of a good. When the stock of a certain good increases, the seller will have to lower the price to get rid of all his goods: richer buyers will then consider satisfying less important desires by buying more goods, and more buyers with a lower willingness to buy will be able to afford the good.

The market price is therefore determined by three elements: the amount of supply, the degree of want or desire, and the purchasing power of the buyers. The market price will therefore go down when more suppliers enter the market, and it will go up when the degree of desire or the purchasing power of the buyers increases. Exchange value can therefore be considered to be subjective, because it is based, for every individual, on the expected use value of the good and on the alternative use value of the money that would have to be given in exchange.

On the other hand, competition between buyers and sellers establishes a market price, which can be seen as exchange value in the objective sense (Wieser 1889: 39–53). Wieser considers the fiction of a perfect communist state in which there is no misuse of power by officials and in which no errors or mistakes are made.[4] This perfectly rational state would distribute the produce in the best possible way:

> Social supply and demand, or amount of goods and utility socially compared with one another, would decide value … That value which arises from the social relation between amount of goods and utility, or value as it would exist in the communist state, we shall henceforth call *Natural Value*. (Wieser 1889: 60)

Exchange value differs from "natural value" because of human imperfection (error, fraud, force, chance) and because of differences between the rich and the poor, which in turn imply differences in purchasing power: "In natural value goods are estimated simply according to their marginal utility; in exchange value, according to a combination of marginal utility and purchasing power" (Wieser 1889: 62). This implies, for instance, that according to natural value, luxuries would be valued less and necessities more than they are in exchange value. Wieser needs this concept of "natural value" to investigate the principles of imputation, or the individual valuation of the contribution of different factors of production to the final product.

The problem of imputation arises because different factors of production – such as land, labour and capital – are typically combined to produce a given final product.[5] We can clearly determine the combined effect of these factors (the marginal utility of the final product), but we need to know the individual contribution of each factor. As we saw before, Menger argued that we need to imagine by how much the value would decrease when a certain factor of production is taken away. For instance, we could compare

---

4. It is clear that Wieser has no sympathy at all for communism or socialism: "In its simplicity, purity, and originality it is so attractive, and at the same time so contradictory to all experience, that it is doubtful whether it can ever be more than a dream" (Wieser 1889: 61). Socialist writers, such as Karl Marx, typically build their analysis on the labour theory of value, which according to Wieser is completely wrong: "The origin of value, which lies in utility and not in labour, is mistaken" (Wieser 1889: 66).

5. Note that Wieser does not accept the "abstinence" explanation for profits, brought forward by earlier economists such as John Stuart Mill. The value of capital is not derived from the fact that capitalists do not consume their capital, even if it were straightforward to simply turn capital into consumption (which it typically is not, since all the capital goods would first need to be sold). Valuation must follow the principles of marginalism, and "abstinence from consumption is nothing more than a symptom of productive value" (Wieser 1889: 166–8).

the produce from a piece of land when manure has been used and when it has not. Wieser, however, states that "the deciding element is not that portion of the return which is lost through the loss of a good, but that which is secured by its possession" (Wieser 1889: 85). The value of the manure is not determined by the decrease in production that would occur if we did not use the manure but by the increase in production from using it.

However, every factor of production not only "contributes" to the final product, it also "cooperates" with other factors of production. If a farmer has to work without manure, then the value of the final product is lower. But not only will the value decrease because manure was not used, the absence of manure will also make the contribution of the land and that of the labour smaller. In order to resolve this issue, Wieser wants to set up a system of equations.[6] As has been remarked by several authors, Wieser's system of equations, even if they could be established, does not solve the problem of distribution.[7]

Wieser concludes that the "marginal law", which states that the value of a stock of identical goods is determined by the marginal utility of the good, i.e. the use value derived from the good that is used to satisfy the least important desires, also applies to a stock of means of production. The "marginal product" of a means of production is determined by the contribution to the final product by the last dose that is applied, or, therefore, by the dose that is applied in the least productive circumstances.

For instance, on a given piece of land there are diminishing returns to labour (see chapter 2). Suppose that there are currently nine labourers working on this piece of land, and that they produce 100kg of potatoes in

---

6. Wieser suggests that we would have to set up a system of equations with the different combinations of the factors of production on the left-hand side and the value of the jointly acquired returns on the right-hand side. If we have the three equations $x + y = 100$, $2x + 3z = 290$ and $4y + 5z = 590$, where x, y and z are our different factors of production, then elementary mathematics leads us to conclude that $x = 40$, $y = 60$ and $z = 70$.

7. See, in particular, Pullen (2010: 17–19). Pullen's critical review of the marginal productivity theory of distribution, which goes beyond the scope of this introductory discussion, argues that it is impossible to precisely disentangle the specific marginal products of the various factors of production. If this is the case, then no normative conclusions can be drawn from this theory, which means that it cannot justify why certain factors, such as capital and labour, gain a certain reward given their contribution to the final product (which cannot be established). Pullen argues that the marginal productivity theory of distribution should be replaced by a bargaining power theory of distribution.

total. Suppose that adding a tenth labourer would increase the output to 105kg of potatoes. The marginal product of labour is then 5kg of potatoes. By adding more labourers to the piece of land, the marginal product of labour will go down. For instance, adding the eleventh labourer to the piece of land would increase output to 108kg, and therefore the marginal product of the eleventh labourer is equal to only 3kg. Of course, the same labourer could be used on a different piece of land, or even in a completely different sector (such as manufacturing). If a factor can be used in several different processes of production, then we do not necessarily need to achieve equality of the "marginal amount", since the "scales of satisfaction" may be quite different. This argument is similar to Wieser's interpretation of Gossen's second law, which we discussed above.

Wieser illustrates this with gold, which could be used to produce luxury goods but also to fill teeth – it would be impossible to achieve the same marginal amount for both activities. Therefore, at any given moment in time, it does not need to be the case that all utilities are adjusted to the marginal level. For instance, if iron were used for three different purposes A, B and C, where one unit of iron leads to a marginal utility of 10, 9 and 8, respectively, then the "marginal return" for iron would be equal to 8 (i.e. derived from the purpose with the lowest marginal utility). This would occur at a stage of production where not all utilities are adjusted to the marginal level, since the processes A and B yield marginal utility higher than 8. But given that purpose A yields the highest return, it is quite likely that, over time, the supply of A would increase, and that the marginal utility of A would therefore decrease (Wieser 1889: 96–100). Obviously, the supply of C would decrease and the marginal utility of C would increase. This is again a good illustration of the Austrian "process" approach, which differs substantially from the mainstream "equilibrium" approach. There is no static equilibrium at any given moment in time, but significant differences in valuations will set in motion a process by which individual producers switch to the most lucrative processes (which typically takes time).

We can conclude that Austrian writers such as Menger and Wieser provide an interesting and alternative view of marginalism, compared with "equilibrium" writers such as Jevons and Walras. There is no equilibrium at any point in time, since the world is constantly in flux. The Austrians are mainly interested in the processes of decision-making by rational individuals who want to improve their levels of satisfaction in a changing world of imperfect information. But they agree with Jevons and Walras that value is determined by the conditions prevailing at the margin. The Austrians also emphasize the role of time in the production process and in the determination of value. This is also the case for Alfred Marshall, whose *Principles of Economics* will be considered in the next chapter. Marshall's work is often seen as a synthesis of previous economic theory, but he also introduces period analysis and the important concept of "consumer surplus". We will also discuss the writings of John Bates Clark, who provides an elaborate static model of marginalist economic theory. It turns out that using marginalist principles, the theory of rent can be turned into a general theory of income distribution.

7

Alfred Marshall, John Bates Clark and the marginalist synthesis

Cambridge scholar Alfred Marshall is recognized as the most important British economist of the late nineteenth and early twentieth century. Not only was he versed in the works of classical economists such as Smith and Ricardo, he was also familiar with the writings of lesser-known Continental European writers such as Thünen and Cournot. Furthermore, he also knew the works of the marginalist authors Jevons, Walras and Menger. His extensive knowledge of the existing economics literature enabled him to provide a unified view on economic theory, to which he added the important notion of "consumer surplus" and, with his period analysis, the role of time in economic theory. Marshall's *Principles of Economics* (1890) became the leading textbook in economic theory and in it he attempted "to present a modern version of the old doctrines with the aid of the new work" (Marshall 1890: xi).

> Under the guidance of Cournot, and in a less degree of von Thünen, I was led to attach great importance to the fact that our observations [...] relate not so much to aggregate quantities, as to increments of quantities, and that in particular the demand for a thing is a continuous function, of which the *marginal* increment is, in stable equilibrium, balanced against the corresponding increment of its cost of production. (Marshall 1890: xvi)

Marshall's work can be seen as a synthesis of classical and mathematical economic theory, guided by the principle of marginalism. In this chapter, we will first consider Marshall's views on wealth, value and utility and examine his period analysis. We will then explore his notion of "consumer surplus", which paves the way for economic welfare theory (to be investigated in the next chapter). Marshall realized that there is a strong similarity between the theory of rent and consumer surplus, which he originally named "consumer's rent". This idea was taken up by the American economist John Bates Clark, who extends the theory of rent to become a general economic theory of income distribution. We will describe his static view of the economic system, in which the distribution of income is determined by the theory of rent and by the principles of marginalism. The chapter closes with a review of Clark's attempt to turn this system into a normative theory – one that not only explains the distribution of income, but also justifies it.

Wealth, value and utility

According to Marshall, wealth consists of all things that can satisfy human needs directly or indirectly, including material as well as non-material goods. Hence, these "things" may be either goods or services provided by human labour. Value is simply exchange value, which tells us what the relationship is between particular goods (or services) at a particular place and time. In advanced economies this exchange value is typically expressed in terms of money, which then becomes the price of goods.[1] Since economic transactions are driven by desires or wants, "utility" must play a central role in economic theory, and the precise relationship between "exchange value" and "utility" needs to be determined. The total utility of a stock of goods increases with every increase in stock, but at a diminishing rate. If a consumer hesitates about adding a further unit to his existing stock of goods, then he will consider the "marginal utility" of this additional good, which may then result in a "marginal purchase".

Marshall reformulates Gossen's first law as follows: "The marginal utility of a thing to anyone diminishes with every increase in the amount of it he already has" (Marshall 1890: 93). He emphasizes that this is only valid if the "character" and "tastes" of the individual remain constant: for instance,

---

1. Marshall chooses to ignore changes in the general purchasing power of money (inflation or deflation), since his work is focused on the "foundations" of economics and should therefore ignore this difficulty (Marshall 1890: 54–62).

listening to good music may increase the taste for music and would there-fore increase its marginal utility.[2]

Gossen's first law can also be translated in terms of price. The larger the stock of a certain good in somebody's possession, the lower the price he would be willing to pay for an additional unit will be, everything else remain-ing equal: this price can be called the "marginal demand price". The demand will only become "efficient" if the marginal demand price reaches the price at which others are willing to sell. With these conceptions Marshall connects the notion of "utility" with the notion of "exchange value" or "price", which allows him to draw a demand curve (Figure 7.1).

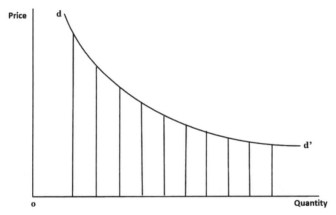

Figure 7.1 Marshall's demand curve.
Source: Marshall (1890: 96).

This demand curve explains the "law of demand" – that the quantity of a good that is demanded will increase if the price of the good decreases – in terms of Gossen's first law of diminishing marginal utility (Marshall 1890: 92–7). The "law of demand" is not simply an observation from facts: it can

---

2. This issue is investigated further by Stigler & Becker (1977: 78), who argue that prefer-ences should be seen as stable, but that changes in human capital matter: "An increase in this music capital [caused by listening to good music] increases the productivity of time spent listening to or devoted in other ways to music." By becoming educated in music, the consumer will derive more enjoyment from listening to music. This increase in productivity would therefore increase the marginal utility of listening to music for the consumer.

be explained by the principles of marginalism. Since the marginal utility of a good decreases when more units of the good are added to the stock of a consumer, he or she will only add additional units to the stock if the marginal demand price goes down. Hence, when the price goes down, the quantity demanded will go up. Total demand (or "aggregate" demand, as economists like to say) for a good is the sum of the demand from all the individual consumers. While these individuals will be different in terms of taste and purchasing power,

> the peculiarities in the wants of individuals will compensate one another in a comparatively regular gradation of total demand. Every fall, however slight, in the price of a commodity in general use, will, other things being equal, increase the total sales of it.
> (Marshall 1890: 98)

This change in quantity demanded, following a decrease in price, may be substantial or moderate, depending on whether the decrease in marginal utility occurs at a faster or slower pace.[3]

Marshall also reformulates Gossen's second law, in order to discuss situations in which one and the same good or service can be used for different purposes: "If a person has a thing which he can put to several uses, he will distribute it among these uses in such a way that it has the same marginal utility in all" (Marshall 1890: 117).[4] Finally, Marshall considers the choice between present and future pleasures. A "discount" must be applied to the future pleasures, because there is uncertainty about the future (an objective property) and different people have different estimations of the future value of a pleasure compared with its present value (a subjective property) (Marshall 1890: 117–23).

---

3. Marshall introduces the notion of "elasticity" (or responsiveness) of demand following a change in price. For example, the elasticity of salt is very low: if the price of salt is lowered, the consumption of salt will hardly increase. A lower price for necessities such as butter and medical services will have a great impact on the quantity demanded by the poor but the rich will probably not markedly change their personal consumption (Marshall 1890: 102–13).

4. Marshall uses domestic production, rather than domestic consumption, as an example: yarn that can be applied to produce either socks or vests. He argues that there are typically fewer alternative uses for the consumption of a good, and that Gossen's second law is "less important and less interesting" for the demand side than for the supply side.

So far, Marshall's writings are clearly in line with the works of earlier authors such as Jevons and Walras. As we discussed above (and in earlier chapters), there is a clear relationship between marginal utility and value. But whereas Jevons was particularly hostile towards classical authors such as Ricardo, who postulated that there is a clear relationship between cost of production and value, Marshall takes a different approach. For him, the contrast between a marginal utility theory and a cost of production theory of value is clarified when the time period is taken into consideration. Marshall unifies both approaches: "We might as reasonably dispute whether it is the upper or the under blade of a pair of scissors that cuts a piece of paper, as whether value is governed by utility or cost of production" (Marshall 1890: 164).

Both factors play an important role in the determination of value, depending on the time period that is taken into consideration. For a very short time period, e.g. one day, the supply is usually fixed. If a farmer brings her products, such as fresh vegetables, to the market, then she must sell them on the same day, otherwise her stock would spoil. In such a situation, demand, and therefore utility, will have a strong impact on the (exchange) value (and therefore market price). If lots of consumers attach a high marginal utility to the vegetables, then the farmer will be able to charge high prices. If this is not the case, then she will have to be satisfied with much lower prices. Since the time period is very short (one day), the farmer cannot simply increase or decrease his supply in order to influence the market price, and therefore the price will be determined mainly by demand and, therefore, by marginal utility.

For a longer period, e.g. several years, supply can be changed at will. If the demand for a good increases, then the market price will rise, and hence producers will find it profitable to produce a larger supply. Next year (or next harvest), the farmers will appear on the market with a larger supply of vegetables. Consequently, the market price will fall again to the "normal" level, which is equal to the cost of production. Therefore, the long-run equilibrium price of a good will be equal to its cost of production; when these costs go down, the long-run equilibrium price will follow.

Marshall therefore concludes that utility will have the strongest influence on value in the short run, and that cost of production becomes more important when the time period increases. Higher marginal valuations will increase demand, and lower costs of production will increase supply. But the effect of changes in demand (utility) are immediate, whereas it takes time to change production and supply following an alteration in the costs of production (Marshall 1890: 164–6).

In other words, Marshall unifies the "classical" cost of production approaches of Smith and Ricardo with the "marginalist" value approaches of Jevons, Walras and Menger. Marginalist economic theory is focused on the short run, when supply is relatively fixed, and therefore the exchange value or price of a good is determined by the marginal valuations of the consumers. Higher marginal valuations imply a higher market price. When the time period lengthens, the supply can be adjusted to the changing demand (because this takes time). The market price of a good will then fluctuate around its cost of production, which the classical authors named the "natural price" of the good. If the market price exceeds this "natural price", then suppliers benefit from an increased profit margin. They will find it beneficial to produce more units, and supply will increase (eventually) and hence the market price will again decrease. The profit margin will also increase when the costs of production go down, which will therefore have a similar effect on supply and market price. Depending on the industry, this process of adjustment of supply may happen at a faster or at a slower pace.

Smith and Ricardo were also right, but they examined the long-run equilibrium price of a competitive economy. The "scissors" metaphor implies that the "marginalist" blade of utility cuts deeper in the short run, whereas the "classical" blade of cost of production cuts deeper in the long run. But both blades are required to cut the paper, and both marginal utility and cost of production are required to understand the establishment of the market price.

Consumer surplus

We have seen above that a consumer will purchase additional units of a certain good until its marginal utility becomes equal to the given market price, and that the marginal utility declines as more units are consumed or are added to the stock. This also implies that the units purchased before the last unit had a marginal utility that was higher than the market price. Since all these units were bought at the same price, the consumer made some kind of "profit" on the earlier units compared with the later units. In order to discuss this phenomenon, Marshall introduced the notion of "consumer's surplus", which claims a central place in microeconomic theory, particularly in the economic analysis of welfare. His reasoning is similar to Dupuit's arguments about the measurement of utility (discussed in chapter 3). Marshall presents a numerical example to illustrate this "consumer surplus", as it is called in modern microeconomics:

Suppose that a man is willing to buy one pound of tea at a price of 20 shillings, and that if the price goes down to 14 shillings, he would be willing to buy two pounds. Given that he wants to pay 20 shillings for the first pound of tea, the satisfaction that he derives from this first pound must at least be equal to 20 shillings. The additional utility of the second pound must at least be equal to 14 shillings, since he buys a second unit at this lower price. Therefore, the total utility derived from the first and second pounds of tea must at least be equal to 20 shillings + 14 shillings = 34 shillings, whereas he only paid 28 shillings to acquire two pounds of tea. His consumer surplus in this case is therefore equal to 34 shillings – 28 shillings = 6 shillings.

The consumer surplus rises when the price declines further: to 10 shillings, for instance. If the consumer is willing to acquire three pounds of tea at a price of 10 shillings, then his total utility must be at least equal to 20 shillings + 14 shillings + 10 shillings = 44 shillings, whereas he only paid 30 shillings to acquire three pounds. His consumer surplus in this case is therefore 44 shillings – 30 shillings = 14 shillings. This can be illustrated graphically with a demand curve (Figure 7.2).

At a price of o–c (measured on the y-axis), the consumer is willing to acquire o–h units (measured on the x-axis). His total expenditure is then given by the rectangular area c–o–h–a, which represents the price (o–c) multiplied by the quantity (o–h). The satisfaction derived from the last unit consumed (the h-th unit) must be at least equal to the purchase price (o–c), otherwise the consumer would not have been willing to purchase o–h units. But Gossen's first law implies that the "earlier" units (the units between o and h) must give him a higher utility than the market price o–c, which is obviously the same for all units. For example, at a price of m–p he would have been willing to acquire o–m units, and therefore the value of the m-th unit is worth at least m–p. At the lower price o–c he would only pay o–c for this m-th unit, and thus he gets a benefit of o–r = m–p – o–c. He therefore derives a utility "surplus" from these "earlier units", which is very high for the first unit and then declines to zero for the h-th unit.

The total utility derived from consuming o–h units is then given by the area d–o–h–a, and since his total expenditure is the rectangle c–o–h–a, his consumer surplus is equal to d–o–h–a minus c–o–h–a, which is the area d–c–a.

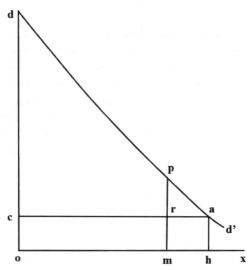

Figure 7.2 Marshall's consumer surplus.
Source: Marshall (1890: 128).

This notion of "consumer surplus" has important implications for the study of total welfare at the society level. All consumers pay the same market price for a specific good, e.g. tea. Suppose that, at a price of 10 shillings, a rich person buys three pounds of tea, whereas a poor person can only purchase one pound of tea. The numerical example above implies that the rich person would have a consumer surplus of at least 14 shillings, whereas the poor person would get, at best, a very small consumer surplus (if he had been willing to pay slightly more than 10 shillings for a pound of tea). In other words, because the rich and the poor pay the same market price for a certain good, the rich will derive more consumer surplus (and thus utility) from the purchase than the poor: "a pound's worth of satisfaction to an ordinary poor man is a much greater thing than a pound's worth of satisfaction to an ordinary rich man" (Marshall 1890: 130). This must be kept in mind by policy-makers when they devise taxation schemes. We will elaborate on this matter when we examine the contribution to welfare economics of Arthur Cecil Pigou (1877–1959), who was a student of Marshall's.[5]

Rent, quasi-rent and marginalism

The notion of "consumer surplus" can also be related to the theory of rent. According to Ricardo, rent is the income that landowners derive from their fertile land. This income is explained by differential gains: a unit of capital-and-labour will yield a higher output in more productive circumstances than it would in less productive conditions, and every unit of output will be sold at the same price. Therefore, farmers compete with each other to acquire the most productive circumstances and therefore bid up the price of land, which becomes the rent income for the landowner.

Today we tend to use the term "rent" in a very broad way, typically to indicate fixed regular payments that must be made by the borrower of a piece of land, a house or a machine to the lender (owner) of the object. Marshall argues that the word "rent" should be restricted to denoting income that is derived from the free gifts of nature, in particular land; all other forms of "rent" should be referred to as "quasi-rent" (Marshall 1890: 74–5). This distinction is necessary because there is an important difference between the rent paid for a piece of land and other forms of rent. Since the powers of the soil are typically indestructible, ownership of a piece of land guarantees a permanent income. All other forms of "rent" are essentially temporary:

---

5. Marshall recognizes that there is a technical difficulty in his approach: if a person spends more money on any good, then the marginal utility of money will go up for this person (since he will have less money left after the purchase). This will, however, only be important in very rare cases: typically, basic subsistence goods consumed by the poor. As was indicated by the Scottish economist Robert Giffen (1837–1910), a rise in the price of bread has a substantial impact on the budget of the poor, since they spend a large portion of their income on this basic food product. Rather than spending less on bread (which is what would normally be expected following a rise in the price of bread), the marginal utility of money may rise so much that the poor may decide to curtail the consumption of more luxurious food products (such as meat) and may end up spending even more on bread than before it went up in price (Marshall 1890: 132). Such goods – for which quantity demanded increases following a rise in price – are called "Giffen goods" in modern microeconomic theory (and are not generally considered to be very important, if indeed they exist at all). Jensen & Miller (2008) provide evidence of Giffen behaviour for rice (and weaker evidence for wheat) in two provinces of China.

buildings and machines wear out, they can be destroyed or can become obsolete. And if a specific building or machine yields high levels of rental income, then you might expect that more of these buildings or machines will be produced. As the supply of these buildings or machines goes up, the rent must come down. This, of course, is not possible with land or other free limited resources provided by nature: they do not normally wear out, but they can also not be reproduced. However, a wider application of the term "rent" leads to interesting insights for economic theory, as was already indicated by Jevons (see chapter 5).

In the earlier editions of his *Principles of Economics*, Marshall used the term "consumer's rent" rather than "consumer surplus". This is no surprise, given the similarities between these concepts, which are evident in the similarities between the different tables and graphs that we have depicted in previous chapters. Menger's utility Scala (chapter 6) is similar to the table used by Mark Blaug to illustrate the Ricardian theory of rent (chapter 2). The utility curves of Gossen (chapter 3) and Jevons (chapter 4), Jevons's graph to discuss the theory of rent (chapter 4) and Marshall's diagram of consumer surplus (this chapter) all look very similar (although there are also some major differences).[6] The curves are sloping downward because of diminishing returns or diminishing marginal utility: adding more units of capital-and-labour to a piece of land yields diminishing returns; and Gossen's first law implies that the marginal utility curve is a downward slope.

A second similarity between these curves and concepts results from the law of one price. Given that all agricultural products are sold at the same price, those units of capital-and-labour that are utilized in better circumstances yield a higher rent than the units that are utilized in the worst circumstances. The value of a stock of similar goods is determined by the marginal utility of the good (i.e. the utility of the unit that was added "last" to the stock) multiplied by the number of goods in the stock, even though the units that were added "before" had a higher marginal utility. The consumer can derive a surplus because he pays the same market price for all

---

6. The curves of Gossen and Jevons are marginal utility curves, and Marshall's consumer surplus graph represents a demand curve. The demand curve is, however, downward sloping because of diminishing marginal utility, as this explains why the price must fall in order to increase the quantity demanded. Both utility and demand curves are therefore downward sloping for the same reason: Gossen's first law of diminishing marginal utility.

units, while his willingness to pay for his "earlier" units was higher than his willingness to pay for the "last" unit.[7] Marshall emphasizes, however, that it is not true that the marginal use of a thing "governs" the value of the whole. The point is that we need to "go to the margin to study the action of those forces which govern the value of the whole" (Marshall 1890: 226). The margin is actually the state beyond which no further gains in utility or profit are possible; it is the most efficient outcome (everything else remaining the same). This idea is explored further by the American economist John Bates Clark, who presented a theory of distribution as determined by the law of rent.

Clark on the law of rent

> The law of rent has become an obstacle to scientific progress: it has retarded the attainment of a true theory of distribution. Yet it is itself capable of affording such a theory. (Clark 1891: 289)

This is the opening statement of Clark's article, which appeared in 1891 in the *Quarterly Journal of Economics*. Clark starts from a static view of society, which means that all dynamic forces must be eliminated. In particular, he assumes that

- there are no changes in the character of social wants;
- there are no technological changes;
- there are no changes in the organization of industry;
- labour and capital do not shift from one place to another; and
- the amount of labour and capital that is available in the economic system remains constant.

By eliminating all these dynamic forces, Clark ends up with a static view of society in which all means of production (labour and capital) are allocated optimally: if we were to move one unit of labour and capital to a different place in the system, we would reduce total output.

---

7. We will clarify the notions of units that were added "earlier" or "later" in our discussion of John Bates Clark below.

If this equilibrium were disturbed (for whatever reason), then dynamic opportunities for profit are created. For instance, anyone bringing a new product to the market, or implementing a new technology, may secure what Clark calls "pure profit" (at least temporarily, until his competitors have caught up). Therefore, by reducing the dynamic economy to a static condition, we eliminate the possibility of pure profit. Clark argues that this is still a realistic proposition, since static forces are said to be dominant in business (Clark 1891: 289–90). In such a static economy, a certain rate of interest will prevail, e.g. 3 per cent. If there were forms of capital that yielded a higher rate of interest, e.g. 6 per cent, then dynamic forces would come into action. More money would go into purchasing capital to be used in the more lucrative part of the economy, and supply in that section would therefore increase. This would lower the price in that part of the economy, and the rates of interest would therefore be equalized.

As we have seen before (in chapter 1), this is the invisible hand mechanism, which was proposed by Adam Smith. But if you reduce the economy to a static condition, how is the general interest rate of 3 per cent to be explained? Why is it not 2 per cent or 4 per cent in any given static state of the economy (in which the possibility of dynamic forces, such as the invisible hand, is excluded)?

To answer this, Clark argues that the theory of rent may provide an explanation. As we have seen (in chapter 2), labour used in the least productive conditions (such as farming the least fertile land) does not generate any rent, and therefore earns only wages. This is marginal labour, which provides the general standard of pay for all units of labour: one unit of labour is similar to another, and the law of one price implies that all units of labour must be rewarded with the same wage. Extensive rent is generated when lands of different qualities are taken into cultivation, and intensive rent emerges when more units of labour are put on a given piece of land. The "first" units of labour put on the land will generate a higher produce than the "last" units, and these differential gains will become rent income for the landowner because of competition between the labourers. Everybody would like to work in the most productive conditions, and hence the price of land is bid up.

Clark emphasizes the similarity between Ricardo's theory of rent and Marshall's theory of consumer surplus (see above). Because of the law of diminishing returns, the "earlier" purchases will provide a higher utility than "later" purchases. Since the price will be the same for all units, "earlier" purchases will therefore generate a rent for the consumer. But since we have reduced the system to a static condition, it makes no sense to speak of "first" or "last" units of labour, or "earlier" or "later" purchases: any labourer or any unit of purchase may be first or last. For instance, in a restaurant we may choose a menu consisting of a starter and a main dish. The more substantial main dish will provide more utility than the starter, and if both are priced the same, the main dish will provide a "rent" compared with the starter.

When it comes to labour supply, the temporal ordering does matter: the first hours worked will be less painful than the last hours on the job.[8] Hence, if the labourer increases his amount of labour by one or more units, which we can refer to as "increments", differential gains are generated: "Earlier increments bring the same wages, and cost the worker less. They afford a differential gain that we may term labourer's subjective rent" (Clark 1891: 296). The sum of these differential gains, for all but the last hour of the working day, is rent for the labourer, just as the sum of all the differential gains (differences in marginal utilities) for all but the "last" unit consumed is rent for the consumer. The last unit does not provide a differential gain, since for the last unit of labour the wage is equal to the marginal disutility of labour, and for the "last" unit consumed the marginal utility is equal to the price.

These considerations are about the actions of individual landowners, labourers or consumers. We may define "social income" as the total sum of wages and interest in a society. At the level of a society, or as economists like to say, at the aggregate level, we can state that the total sum of all wages is the income derived from the "fund of pure [human] energy". Likewise, aggregate interest is the product of a "fund of pure capital" (Clark 1891: 299–303). A similarity between these funds and a given piece of land emerges: diminishing returns will set in. If you add a labourer to a given piece of land on which two people are already working, then the produce will increase, but not proportionally. Similarly, if the fund of pure capital is fixed, then adding additional labourers will increase production, but at a decreasing rate. The same is true for a fixed fund of pure energy (labour): adding more units of capital (e.g. spades) will increase production, but also at a decreasing rate. Diminishing returns emerge when, in a case of two (or

---

8. See chapter 4 for a further discussion of the supply of labour (according to Jevons).

more) means of production, one of them is fixed in amount and you add more units of the other. Obviously, diminishing returns would not occur if all means of production increase at the same rate.[9]

Returning to the example of land and labour: the last labourer added to a given piece of land will earn wages only; the earlier workers will generate a surplus that will become rent appropriated by the landowner. With a fixed fund of pure capital we get the same result: "Each earlier worker creates a surplus over and above the amount created by the last one, and the sum of all these surpluses is the rent of the fund" (Clark 1891: 305). This rent is equal to aggregate interest, and the rate of interest is then determined by dividing the rent of the fund by the total amount of the fund.

The question now becomes: why is the last man earning wages only? For the landowner, the answer is clear. There are multiple possible employments, and a general wage rate is established for the economy as a whole. The land-owner will employ additional labourers as long as his marginal revenue (the price that he gets for the additional produce) exceeds his marginal cost. This marginal cost is the wage rate of the labourer, which is determined not by the landowner's farm, but by the "outside" economy as a whole (all industrial sectors taken together). This explains why the last worker earns wages only and does not generate any rent: if the worker were to generate more additional revenue than his wage cost, established in the general labour market, then the landowner would be willing to hire more workers. For the fixed fund of pure capital, however, the situation is different: there is no "outside" economy in which the wage rate is determined.

Furthermore, Clark looks at the problem from a static point of view, whereas "adding" labourers to the existing fund is a dynamic process:

> In a static view of the system, we abandon the conception of a working force gradually enlarging, as it was made to do in our illustration. Capital and working force are both fixed in amount through the period that we consider. There is no particular man who is the last to arrive in point of time, but any one may become the final man by giving up his work for a few days and then applying for it again. (Clark 1891: 308)

---

9. If all means of production were to increase at the same rate, then we would speak of "(dis)economies of scale". We will explore this matter further in the next chapter.

The economy must first be reduced to a static state, by eliminating the opportunities for pure profit. Given a fixed fund of pure capital, we can remove one labourer from the system and let him stop working but continue eating. After the removal of this worker, the resources (other labourers and capital) are rearranged in the most optimal way. Given that every labourer may be the marginal worker, the diminution of social income that results from this removal will indicate the marginal product of labour, which forms the standard for the wage rate (since all units of labour are identical and the law of one price prevails). Competition between employers will ensure that the marginal man gets the marginal product as a wage. All earlier increments will provide a surplus, which is a true differential product (the difference between the product of the earlier increment and the product of the last increment).

The same may be done for the rate of interest: given a fixed fund of human energy (labour), we eliminate one unit of capital from the system and investigate by how much social income decreases. This tells us what the marginal product of capital will be, and this provides the basis for determining the rate of interest. Both the aggregate amount of wages and the aggregate amount of interest are rents, consisting of the sum of all differential gains. This also implies that Ricardo's theory of rent is not a true differential product, since the value of the marginal labour is not determined within the system, but by reference to the outside world of industry, in which a general wage rate prevails. If we take the total funds of human energy or pure capital into account, then there is no "outside" world in which the wage rate or the interest rate could be determined. Starting from a fixed capital fund, we can determine the wage by removing the marginal worker (which could be any worker) from the system; starting from a fixed labour fund, we can determine the rate of interest by removing the marginal unit of capital (which could be any unit). Using marginalist principles, we can therefore conclude that both the aggregate amount of wages and the aggregate amount of interest are forms of rent, to be explained by differential gains (Clark 1891: 308–12).

From positive to normative

Clark's *The Distribution of Wealth* (1899) elaborates on the "natural law" that determines the distribution of income of society: which part goes to wages, interest and profits? At the society level, we need to look into aggregate amounts: general wages, general interest and aggregate profits. Clark's general thesis states that "where natural laws have their way, the share of income that attaches to any productive function is gauged by the actual product of it" (Clark 1899: 3). In other words, perfect competition guarantees that all factors of production are rewarded according to their marginal product: the wage is determined by the marginal product of labour and the interest rate is determined by the marginal product of capital. He does not claim to determine what every individual person will get, as personal incomes are typically the result of a mixture of sources: labourers receive wages for their labour, but also own some capital; capitalists derive interest from their capital but also perform labour; and entrepreneurs earn profits (by coordinating), but also perform labour and own capital.

Clark wants to fix the general wage rate, the general rate of interest and the general rate of net profits: what an individual earns will then be determined by the amount of labour that he performs, the amount of capital that he provides, and the amount of coordination that he undertakes. He regards this as a "functional study", leading to certain "rules" of distribution, which he sees as completely distinct from ethics. Some socialists may argue that these rules lead to a distribution that does not conform to justice, and that some corrections have to be made: part of the product should be taken from some people (e.g. interest from capitalists) and given to others (to increase wages for the labourers). This would imply, however, the violation of property rights. Clark does not want to enter the realm of ethics and only considers "natural distribution" (Clark 1899: 8).

Following his earlier approach, Clark investigates the economy under static conditions. Dynamic changes – such as population increases, capital increases, technological progress, changes in consumer desires, and the replacement of less efficient businesses with more efficient ones – are excluded. These changes would alter the structure of the system, which consists of several industrial groups. Each group (named A, B, C) uses labour and capital to transform raw materials into intermediary goods, and these again are transformed into products for consumers. For instance, cattle may be denoted by A, hides in a warehouse are A', tanned leather is A", and finally A''' denotes leather shoes, ready for consumption. B may be the fleece of a sheep, which becomes woollen garments B''' after a series of transformations. C may be wheat that is eventually turned into bread, C''' (Clark 1899:

56–7). From a dynamic point of view, it could be the case that consumers want more and better shoes (A'''). The price of shoes will then increase, and both labour and capital used in shoe production will gain a premium on wages and interest. Entrepreneurs will shift labour and capital (taken from groups B and C) to this industry (A), and therefore the supply of shoes will increase and the price will go down again, annihilating the premium. We are back in a static state, in which, as we have seen above, entrepreneurial profits are reduced to zero. Clark does not deny the existence of dynamic forces, but he claims that static forces are "dominant in the midst of disturbances" (Clark 1899: 67).

Clark argues that the "natural prices" of classical political economy are essentially "static prices". If all dynamic forces are excluded, then we end up in a "natural condition" in which labour earns a "normal rate of wages" and capital earns a "normal rate of interest" (Clark 1899: 69–70). Clearly, competition is an important prerequisite for this natural condition, as government regulations or monopolies may prevent the establishment of these normal rates. It is also clear that marginalism is responsible for these normal rates: the products of labour and capital in the margin, also called the marginal products of labour and capital, respectively, determine the normal rate of wages and interest.

While Clark explicitly excludes ethical considerations from his analysis, it is also clear that a deviation from these "normal" rates, resulting in excess wages or interest, may be seen as opposite to justice and in violation of property rights. As explored by Leonard (2003), this reasoning led Clark to oppose minimum wage rates, as this would imply that some labourers would receive an income above the marginal product of labour (although setting minima would be acceptable if labourers were paid below the marginal product of labour). Leonard argues that Clark should not be seen as an advocate of capital, nor as a progressive partisan of labour, but rather as an American neoclassical advocating for "efficiency" (Leonard 2003: 522). If wages and interest are indeed in accordance with, respectively, marginal product of labour and marginal product of capital, then all factors of production are allocated optimally and no further gains can be made by rearrangements – we are therefore in the most efficient situation.

Marshall and Clark turned marginalism into a general theory of economics. The value of a good or service is determined by the conditions prevailing at the margin, and the theory of rent becomes a general theory of income determination. While Marshall is sometimes described as an evolutionary economist (see, for example, Raffaelli 2002), Clark can be seen as an advocate of the marginalist static system. A lot of criticism can be raised against Clark's reasoning: can we actually adequately measure the marginal products of labour and capital – an issue that is explored at length in *The Distribution of Wealth* – and can the contributions of capital and labour to the final product really be disentangled?[10]

The problem of heterogeneous capital in particular has received considerable attention. Clark distinguishes between "capital" and "capital goods": the former is an aggregate, whereas the latter refers to the specific forms (spades, machines, buildings, but also land) in which capital is "imputed". But how is this "heterogeneous capital" to be measured?[11]

Another issue concerns the existence of perfectly competitive conditions. By the late nineteenth century, economists had already recognized that it is not straightforward to assume that perfect competition is the natural state of the economy: the existence of monopolies or oligopolies (a few large firms dominating a market) accounts for deviations from the efficient equilibrium and therefore also from "normal" prices. Monopolists and firms with extensive market power set higher prices and generate higher profits than firms operating in perfect competition. Furthermore, it is questionable whether all industrial activity is really characterized by diminishing marginal returns, which is one of the cornerstones of marginalist theory. We will explore this and other issues in our final chapter, where we further investigate developments and applications of marginalism in the twentieth century.

---

10. See Pullen (2010) for an elaborate criticism of the marginal productivity theory of distribution.
11. This issue has inspired the so-called Cambridge Controversies in Capital Theory: see Cohen & Harcourt (2003) for an overview.

8

Marginalism in the twentieth century

At the beginning of this book, the development of marginalism was described not as a revolution, but as a slow, cumulative process. Many key ideas and theories had already been formulated before the 1870s, when the important works of Jevons, Walras and Menger appeared. But it was in the 1930s that "marginalism" started to gain a central place at the core of economic theory and the newly emerging economic discipline. This process was accompanied by a growing professionalization of the field. Furthermore, the use of mathematics within economic theory had gained general acceptance at around the same time. It was also the era in which methods were developed to measure important economic magnitudes, such as the national income (the total value of all goods and services produced by a nation within a year) and the rate of inflation (the level of price increases within the economy) (see Landreth & Colander 2002: 454–5).

In this chapter we will consider the contribution of "marginalism" to these developments. First, we will examine the extension of the marginalist vocabulary by John Hicks (1904–89) and Roy George Douglas Allen (1906–83). By introducing the notion of the "marginalist rate of substitution", authors could circumvent concerns about the possible measurement and quantification of (marginal) utility. This approach also led to the development of "indifference curves" and "indifference maps", which are now central components of microeconomic theory.

Marshall had realized that economists could not simply take the conditions of "perfect competition" for granted, since markets are often dominated by a small number of large firms, which therefore have substantial market power (though not a monopoly position). In order to deal with markets that are somehow "in between" perfect competition and monopoly, several approaches were developed. We will first examine the theories of imperfect competition that were posited by Joan Robinson (1903–83) and Edward

Hastings Chamberlin (1899–1967). We will then investigate several models that pay closer attention to how exactly firms compete. The model of quantity competition emerged from the writings of Antoine Cournot. The model of price competition emerged from a paper written by the mathematician Joseph Bertrand (1822–1900), which was (ironically enough) intended to be a criticism of the approaches provided by Walras and Cournot. We will also consider the contribution of Heinrich von Stackelberg (1905–46), who developed a sequential model of competition (in which a firm undertakes strategic actions after having observed the actions of its competitor). We will see that marginalism plays a central role in all these theories of imperfect competition.

This is also the case for "welfare economics", a subfield of economics that was also established in the early twentieth century. In order to study economic welfare, Arthur Pigou extended the vocabulary of marginalism with concepts such as "marginal private net product" and "marginal social net product".

Finally, we will consider the development of macroeconomic theory, initiated by John Maynard Keynes (1883–1946). We will see that Keynes's *General Theory* (1936) utilizes several marginalist concepts, even though his approach and his conclusions differ fundamentally from those of earlier marginalist authors.

The marginal rate of substitution and indifference curves

An important development in the field of economics occurred in the 1930s with the introduction of the "marginal rate of substitution" by the British economists John Hicks and Roy George Douglas Allen. As we have seen already in the writings of the earliest marginalists, a tendency towards "cardinal utility" – that is, the idea that "utility" can be measured (see, for example, Gossen) and that a number can be attached to certain utilities (see, for example, Menger's Scala) – is in evidence.[1]

The Italian economist Vilfredo Pareto (1848–1923) abandoned these notions in his *Manual of Political Economy* (first published in 1906, in Italian)

---

1. Note that modern developments in behavioural economics and neuroeconomics suggest that a cardinal utility function may be relevant for economists after all. See Cartwright (2011) for an introduction to these fields.

and he drew the first indifference curve (see below).[2] Hicks (1934: 54) builds on Pareto's work when he argues that the subjective theory of value should be transformed into a "general logic of choice". If total utility cannot be quantified, then marginal utility cannot be quantified either. But Hicks argues that this is not required: we only need to know the "marginal rate of substitution" between any two goods: "The marginal rate of substitution of any good Y for any other good X is defined as the quantity of good Y which would just compensate him for the loss of a marginal unit of X" (Hicks 1934: 55). This "marginal rate of substitution" (MRS) may also be called the "relative marginal utility". If the market prices are given, then in equilibrium the marginal rate of substitution between two goods for a consumer must be equal to the ratio of their prices, since otherwise exchange could still improve the position of the consumer. This can be illustrated with a simple numerical example, as follows.

If a consumer faces a choice between two goods – let us say food and shelter – then we do not need to know the marginal utility of either food or shelter. We instead need to know how many units of shelter would be required to persuade the consumer to give up a unit of food. If a consumer was willing to give up one unit of food in exchange for three units of shelter, then the "marginal rate of substitution" of food would be three (three units of shelter per unit of food). If she would exchange one unit of food for three units of shelter, then the exchange would leave her total utility unchanged. Suppose that food costs €8 per unit whereas shelter costs only €2 per unit. This means that the consumer could exchange one unit of food for four units of shelter in the market. Since her MRS for food in terms of shelter is three, she would be willing to give up one unit of food in exchange for three units of shelter, in order to maintain the same level

---

2. The mathematics (calculus) required for indifference curves was first provided by the Irish economist Francis Ysidro Edgeworth (1845–1926) in his *Mathematical Psychics* (1881). Pareto is nowadays mainly known for the notion of "Pareto optimality" or "Pareto efficiency", which indicates a certain allocation of means, a reallocation of which in order to improve an individual's position is not possible without simultaneously making at least one other person worse off. This does not imply that a "Pareto optimal" allocation is necessarily the "best" possible allocation in every respect: for instance, an allocation in which one person owns everything and everybody else nothing, is still "Pareto optimal" (since every reallocation, even if extremely small, will still make the richest person worse off). Rather, if an allocation is *not* Pareto optimal, then it means that it is still possible to improve economic efficiency, as a reallocation would improve at least one person's situation without making anybody else worse off.

of satisfaction (utility) as before the exchange. But the market will provide her with four units of shelter in exchange for one unit of food: this implies that the market exchange will make her better off than she was before the exchange, since she now has the same level of utility plus the utility from the fourth additional unit of shelter.

If there are many market participants, then one simple act of exchange will not alter relative prices. The same is not true for the MRS of the consumer, since after the exchange she will have less food and more shelter. Following the law of diminishing marginal utility, this implies that, after the exchange, and because of it, the marginal utility of food must have increased, whereas the marginal utility of shelter must have decreased. Therefore, the MRS of food for shelter must have increased: the consumer will now want more than three units of shelter in exchange for one unit of food in order to maintain the same level of satisfaction. Therefore, the consumer will want to continue this exchange as long as her MRS is below the price ratio, and in equilibrium both must be equal.

Hicks argues that the principle of diminishing marginal utility must be replaced by the "increasing rate of marginal substitution": the more units of food that are given up by the consumer, the more units of shelter she will require for further acts of exchange.

The increasing rate of marginal substitution is shown in Figure 8.1, which represents the MRS for a consumer facing a choice between commodities X (e.g. shelter) and Y (e.g. food). In the graph we can see three curves: a curve with a right-angle in it and a straight line (two "extreme cases": see below), and, in between these two, the general shape of an "indifference curve" (Hicks 1934: 57–9). All points on the indifference curve denote bundles of commodities X and Y that will give the consumer the same level of satisfaction or utility. For instance, the consumer may derive the same level of satisfaction by having either two units of good X and three of good Y, or by having one unit of good X and five units of good Y: she is "indifferent" between the two bundles (2,3) and (1,5). All bundles that deliver the same level of satisfaction are on one and the same indifference curve. The curve must be downward sloping: if we increase the amount of commodity X, then we must simultaneously decrease the amount of commodity Y, since we want the level of satisfaction on any given indifference curve to remain constant (the consumer must be "indifferent" between the situations before and after the exchange).

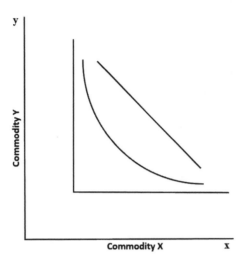

Figure 8.1 Marginal rate of substitution for a consumer facing a choice between two commodities X and Y.

Source: Hicks (1934: 58).

Applied to our numerical example, the consumer with a bundle of two units of X and three units of Y would not mind giving up one unit of X for two units of Y: the new bundle (1,5) will give her the same amount of satisfaction as the original bundle (2,3), and the consumer therefore stays on the same indifference curve.

The curve must also be convex to the origin (curving outwards), which expresses the principle of "increasing marginal rate of substitution" (and therefore also of diminishing marginal utility). This can be explained by consumers' preference for mixtures of goods over extremes: nobody wants to have only food and no shelter, or no food and only shelter. The more food we give up in exchange for shelter, the more shelter we will require for giving up additional units of food, since we will have ever fewer units of food in our possession (and we do not want to live in a palace while starving to death because of a lack of food). The two "extreme" graphs represent the cases of perfect complements and perfect substitutes. The right-angled curve represents perfect complements: left and right shoes, for example. We are not willing to give up left shoes in exchange for right shoes, since we want them in pairs. The only relevant point on the curve is the point at the corner: if we have three left shoes and three right shoes, then adding more left shoes without adding the same amount of right shoes (or vice versa) will not increase our satisfaction. The straight line represents perfect substitutes: an example would be the choice between cups of coffee and cups of tea if we only care about the caffeine content. If the cup of coffee has three times as much caffeine in it than the cup of tea, then we would be willing to give up one cup of coffee for three cups of tea, no matter how many coffees or teas we already had in our possession.

Note that every individual indifference curve represents a certain level of satisfaction or utility; if we were to increase the amount of both goods, then we would end up on a different (higher) indifference curve. We could then draw an "indifference map" (Figure 8.2).

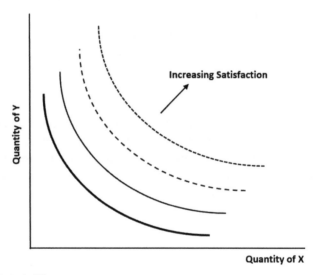

Figure 8.2 An indifference map.
Source: Frank (2013: 82).

The more we move to the right and towards the top, the higher our level of satisfaction will become; the indifference curve on top is "higher" than the indifference curve at the bottom. Of course we could never draw all possible indifference curves, since there are an infinite number of them (having twice the amount of both X and Y will always make us end up on a "higher" indifference curve). Given that, in equilibrium (when utility is maximized), the MRS between two goods must be equal to their relative price ratio, we can find this equilibrium by drawing a budget line, which represents all bundles that can be achieved with a given budget and with given prices, and in doing so find the highest indifference curve that can be achieved.[3] As we saw above, measurement of utility is not required in order to find the optimal choice of the consumer.[4]

The analysis of consumer choice can also be extended to the choice between present and future goods: I may decide to consume less (or more) food in the present, which implies that I will have more (or less) food in the future. This field is now known as "intertemporal choice theory". Its central concept is the "marginal rate of time preference" (MRTP), which grew out of the writings of the Austrian economists Menger and Eugen von Böhm-Bawerk (1851–1914) and was further developed by the American economist Irving Fisher (1867–1947). As we saw before, consumers typically have a preference for the present over the future, so if they give up present goods (today's food), they will require more goods in the future (tomorrow's food) in exchange in order to maintain the same level of satisfaction. MRTP tells us how many future units are required in exchange for a present unit. This MRTP will be different for different consumers, depending on how much they value future consumption compared with present consumption.

A related concept, but now on the production side, is the "marginal rate of technical substitution" (MRTS). If we have two production factors or inputs (labour and capital), then MRTS tells us how many units of capital are required to replace a unit of labour (or vice versa) without changing the level of output. This approach allows us to depict the choice of inputs for a

3. For a "normal" convex utility curve, this implies that the slope of the indifference curve (which is equal to the MRS) must be equal to the slope of the budget line (which is equal to the relative price ratio). The optimal bundle will be found on the highest indifference curve that "touches" the budget line in simply one point. For perfect complements (with indifference curves with a right-angle), we will always end up in the corner of the highest curve that can be achieved with the given budget. For perfect substitutes (straight lines), we will always end up in a corner (the intersection of the highest indifference curve either on the x-axis or on the y-axis, buying only one of the goods), unless the slope of the indifference curves is the same as the slope of the budget line, in which case all bundles on the budget line would give us the same amount of satisfaction.

4. But then the question remains: how can we know the preferences of the consumer? To address this issue, an alternative to utility theory, named "revealed preference theory", was developed by the American economist Paul Samuelson (1915–2009). The consumer reveals his preferences by making a certain choice, in a situation of given market prices and with a given budget.

firm with curves that look like those used in rational consumer choice, but the "indifference curves" are now called "isoquants" (which represent input combinations that yield the same level of output), and the budget line of the consumer corresponds to the "isocost line" of the firm (lines that represent input combinations that have the same total cost).[5] The introduction of central concepts such as MRS, MRTP and MRTS implies that the notions of marginalism pervade the entire field of contemporary microeconomics.

Theories of imperfect competition

Another major development in microeconomic theory during the twentieth century has its origin in the changing nature of competition within markets, which was observed by economists. Several theories of "imperfect competition" were developed in response to this observation. Throughout the nineteenth century, economists would (often tacitly) assume that competitive conditions prevail in markets – modern economists would say that market structures were assumed to be perfectly competitive. Contemporary textbooks in microeconomics typically list four conditions for a market to be perfectly competitive:

1. All firms sell a standardized or homogeneous product – this implies that buyers do not care which seller they buy from as all products are identical.
2. Firms are price takers: they take the market price as a given and do not think that their supply decisions influence the market price. This condition is usually fulfilled when there are many companies on the market, so that no single firm can substantially change the market supply by deciding to offer more or less of their product.
3. There is free entry to and exit from the market for firms: when the profit rate increases, more firms will enter; when the profit rate goes down, some firms will decide to leave the market.
4. Finally, perfect information prevails, for both consumers and firms.

---

5. It would lead us too far to discuss optimal consumer choice and optimal input choice for the firm in detail. The interested reader can find elaborate descriptions in standard textbooks of microeconomics such as Frank and Cartwright (2013).

Given that the goods are homogeneous and that buyers have perfect information, they will always buy from the cheapest seller. A uniform market
price will be established, and sellers who cannot produce at this price will
be forced to leave the market. Economists did, however, realize that there
are tendencies towards monopoly: a situation in which only one firm sells
in a certain market, and therefore has substantial market power. As Adam
Smith (see chapter 1) wrote:

> A monopoly granted either to an individual or to a trading com-
> pany has the same effect as a secret in trade or manufactures. The
> monopolists, by keeping the market constantly under-stocked, by
> never fully supplying the effectual demand, sell their commodities
> much above the natural price ... The price of monopoly is upon
> every occasion the highest which can be got. The natural price, or
> the price of free competition, on the contrary, is the lowest which
> can be taken, not upon every occasion indeed, but for any consider-
> able time together. (Smith 1776: 69)

Cournot (see chapter 5) started his analysis with a monopoly firm and then
moved on to consider duopoly (two large firms) and oligopoly (a few large
firms), but most economists of his time would start from perfect competition and consider monopolies as specific cases.[6]

It may appear reasonable to approach the economy of the nineteenth
century from a perfectly competitive perspective, since most consumer
goods were fairly simple and homogeneous and firms tended to be much
smaller than they are today. However, towards the end of the nineteenth
century, tendencies towards monopoly became more prominent and
began to surface.[7] Much-cited is the Sherman Antitrust Act, established
in the United States in 1890, which was set up to combat anticompetitive

---

6. Interestingly, Luigi Amoroso (1930), an Italian economist (1886–1965) who also wrote
   on imperfect competition during the 1930s, denotes perfect competition as "Ricardo"
   and monopoly as "Cournot".
7. The concentration of capital has been a recurring theme especially in the Marxist literature. For instance, in his seminal work *Das Finanzkapital* (1910), Rudolf Hilferding
   describes not only the tendency for capitalist firms to grow bigger and achieve more
   market power, but also the growing role of banks in the provision of capital to these
   large firms and conglomerates. Monopolization combined with excessive availability of
   capital would fuel imperialism: the world would be divided by the leading powers.

tendencies (such as mergers to reduce competition, or agreements between firms to fix prices or to divide markets between them). Today, competition authorities can issue very high fines if they judge that a firm with substantial market share abuses its dominant position.[8] Modern markets are typically dominated by a small number of very large firms, not by a large number of very small firms that sell similar products. Marketing and branding differentiate consumer goods further, so they become more heterogeneous (or less homogeneous).

The simple tools of perfect competition do not therefore seem adequate to investigate modern markets. Marshall was well aware of the changing nature of modern market economies and discussed them in his *Principles of Economics* (1890), and he later devoted an entire volume to these matters: *Industry and Trade*, first published in 1919.

Alfred Marshall on the economics of industry and trade

Marshall observes that the "representative business unit" has grown in size, both in markets that remained competitive and in markets that came under monopolistic control (Marshall 1919: 178). This growth in the size of businesses could not be explained by diminishing returns, which, as we have seen in previous chapters, are a cornerstone of marginalist economic theory. As Longfield remarked, when we add additional units of labour and capital to a given piece of land, production will increase, but at a decreasing rate. We should therefore refer to this phenomenon as diminishing *marginal* returns, since the production continues to increase, though at a decreasing rate. This was observed in agricultural settings and was explained by the limited availability of fertile land. If this situation prevailed in modern industry, then we would not see businesses growing in size, as the addition of ever more units of capital and labour to the process of production would reduce marginal

---

8. At the time of writing, Google was fined €2.4 billion by the European Commission for violating its antitrust rules with Google Shopping. The EU commissioner Margarethe Verstager states: "What Google has done is illegal under EU antitrust rules. It denied other companies the chance to compete on the merits and to innovate. And most importantly, it denied European consumers a genuine choice of services and the full benefits of innovation." See Kottasova, "EU Slaps Google with Record $2.7 billion fine", 27 June 2017, www.money.cnn.com.

returns. Since the firms decide to grow in size, they must think that this is profitable. We must therefore have *increasing* marginal returns in business or industry, in contrast with *decreasing* marginal returns in agriculture.

As we saw in chapter 2, the condition in agriculture is explained by the limited availability of fertile land. Any increase in demand, caused by a growth in population, must then result in decreasing marginal returns in agriculture, which is equivalent to increasing costs: additional units of capital and labour will produce less additional corn than previous units, which is equivalent to saying that the cost of production of additional units of corn will be higher (in the absence of technological progress or the importation of cheap corn from abroad). In industry, additional units of capital and labour may produce more additional products than previous units: contemporary economists would talk about economies of scale in industry. Economies of scale in industry imply increasing marginal returns and therefore decreasing costs.

According to Marshall, these economies of scale may be specific to either the firm itself, or to the industry, or to the economy as a whole (but external to the firm). A good example of the first case is firms that provide utilities and energy. These firms have very large fixed costs, e.g. in constructing a power plant. If the power plant can supply more customers, then the cost per unit of energy will decrease. The second case concerns investments in the infrastructure of the economy as a whole: better roads, railroad transportation systems, postal services and communication systems reduce the costs for firms to bring their products to the consumer. Therefore, the growth of the economy as a whole implies decreasing costs for a typical firm active in that economy.

The long-term market price will then depend on whether the industry is characterized by increasing returns (decreasing costs) or decreasing returns (increasing costs). Suppose that, for whatever reason, consumer demand for a certain good increases. The immediate effect of an increase in demand will be a rise in price. Given that the higher price implies a higher profit rate, supply will also increase after a while, depending on how long it takes to adjust the process of production. If additional raw material can only be obtained at a greater cost, then this higher cost must result in a higher price. If, on the other hand, there are increasing marginal returns and therefore decreasing costs, then the increase in demand, followed by an increase in supply, must lower cost and therefore price.

This growth in demand will always be gradual, as it will take time for people to learn about the products that have now come within their reach at this lower price. For instance, when electrical appliances became attainable to a wider audience, it took time for consumers to experiment with these new products. In order to study the effect of a fall in price, we need to take the "responsiveness of demand" into account, or its "elasticity", which will be different for different kinds of commodity. When demand increases, firms may fully utilize their internal economies: production will be subdivided between specialized departments, products will become more standardized, and marketing efforts (approaching the most favourable markets) will be improved. When the economy as a whole grows, plants will become more accessible, transportation and communication will be easier, and new methods may be adopted that were developed elsewhere in the economy (Marshall 1919: 185–8).

All this implies that a growing economy, which implies growing demand, will also see a growth in the size of businesses, as was indeed observed by Marshall. This tendency also requires economists to rethink their notions regarding the nature of competition. Marshall sees "perfect competition" and "monopoly" as ideal types, and recognizes that real markets are much more complex, with both competitive and monopolistic tendencies appearing together. But in general, the competitive market price will be lower than the monopoly price given the "invisible hand mechanism" that prevails in perfectly competitive markets: a higher price will imply (after a while) greater supply, and therefore, in turn, a lower price again. A monopolist can simply set a price, given that she does not face competition. The monopolist can choose the price so that her profits are maximized. Whether or not it is profitable to lower the price depends on the double effect of this lower price. On the one hand, a lower price will increase the quantity sold. But on the other hand, the monopolist must also lower the price for the consumers who would have been willing to buy at a higher price (unless the monopolist can price discriminate).[9] The monopolist must therefore maximize her profits by taking this double effect of lower prices into account. The monopoly

---

9. Price discrimination entails charging different prices to different consumers. Pigou (1920: 275–9) indicates that price discrimination can only work if consumers buying at a low price cannot resell the product to consumers that would be required to pay a high price – today we call this "arbitrage". Pigou identifies three degrees of price discrimination. The first degree, which is now named "perfect price discrimination", implies

price will also depend, however, on the nature of the costs. In an increasing-returns industry, which corresponds to decreasing costs, the monopolist will be inclined to lower her price further in order to attract more demand, since a larger scale of production implies lower unit costs. This will not be the case in a decreasing-returns industry (which corresponds to increasing costs), such as the production of a wine with a unique flavour that can only be produced in a certain small area (Marshall 1919: 403–5).

Joan Robinson and Edward Chamberlin on imperfect competition

Building on the work of Marshall, several authors of the 1930s went further in their analysis of monopoly behaviour. In her *The Economics of Imperfect Competition* (1933), Robinson wrote:

> In the older text-books it was customary to set out upon the analysis of value from the point of view of perfect competition. The whole scheme appeared almost homogeneous and it had some aesthetic charm. But somewhere, in an isolated chapter, the analysis of monopoly had to be introduced. This presented a hard, indigestible lump which the competitive analysis could never swallow.
>
> (Robinson 1933: 3)

Although the extreme cases of perfect competition and monopoly are rarely observed in practice, there is very little work on "intermediate cases", where a few large firms dominate a certain market. Robinson argues that every individual firm is a monopolist of its own output, and that we reach perfect competition when a large number of them are selling in a perfect market. In order to analyse markets from a monopolistic point of view, the techniques of marginalism, originally developed within the context

---

charging a different price for every consumer, depending on their willingness to pay. A monopolist who can perfectly price discriminate can extract all consumer surplus and turn it into surplus profits. The second degree concerns quantity discounts: the more units a consumer purchases, the lower the price will be. Such a pricing scheme is sometimes used by utility companies. The third degree entails charging different prices to different groups of consumers, for instance when a movie theatre charges lower prices to minors and retired people.

of perfect competition, need to be adopted. The basic principle is that an individual firm will only undertake an action if this action adds more to the firm's gains than to its losses (Robinson 1933: 3–7).

Robinson's analysis relies on geometry, rather than algebra.[10] She constructs marginal- and average-cost curves and explores their geometrical relationships.[11] She also constructs a demand curve, which will normally be falling (since an increase in sales will be achieved by lowering the price). She then defines the concept "marginal revenue" as the increase in total revenue (which is price multiplied by quantity) for the firm generated by selling an additional unit of output (Robinson 1933: 51). The firm will then increase its output as long as marginal revenue exceeds marginal cost: that is, so long as an additional unit of output would generate more additional revenue than it would generate additional costs. If marginal revenue is below marginal cost, then the firm will be willing to reduce output. It follows that the firm will maximize its profits when marginal revenue is equal to marginal cost.

Since the shape (or rather, the slope) of the demand curve depends on the responsiveness of consumer demand to price, or "elasticity", a relationship can be established between marginal revenue and price elasticity of demand. In general, if consumer demand is not very price elastic (and, therefore, is inelastic) – if it concerns a necessary good for which few substitutes exist, for instance – then the firm can increase its price without losing too many sales.[12] The concept of "marginal revenue" is now widely

---

10. She was heavily criticized by Nichol (1934) for using "school geometry" rather than calculus.

11. When marginal costs are rising, average costs are rising as well: a rising marginal cost implies that newly added units cost more than previous units, and therefore average costs must be rising as well. Conversely, decreasing marginal costs imply decreasing average costs. It can then be shown that the marginal cost curve will intersect the average cost curve in its lowest point (if average costs are first declining and then rising) or in its highest point (if average costs are first rising and then declining).

12. Monopoly power is measured by the Lerner index, following Lerner (1934). The Lerner index defines the degree of monopoly as $(P - C)/P$, where P is the market price and C is marginal cost. In equilibrium profits are maximized, and therefore marginal revenue will be equal to marginal cost. In perfect competition marginal revenue is also equal to price (since firms are price takers), and therefore the Lerner index will be zero. For a monopolist marginal revenue will always be smaller than price (since he will have to lower his price if he wants to sell additional units, including the price for units that sold previously at a higher price), and therefore the Lerner index will be positive. The higher the Lerner index, the more monopoly power exists in the market. The relationship between marginal revenue (MR) and price elasticity of demand (ε) is given by MR

used in microeconomic theory and allows the investigation of the profit-maximizing behaviour of firms in many different market structures (perfect competition and monopoly, as well as "intermediate cases"). The rule that, for profit maximization, marginal revenue has to equal marginal cost has become a somewhat fundamental and universal law of microeconomic theory of the firm.

A related (but independently established) approach to imperfect competition was provided by the American economist Edward Chamberlin in his *The Theory of Monopolistic Competition: A Re-Orientation of the Theory of Value* (1933). Rather than treating perfect competition and monopoly as extreme cases, Chamberlin argues that product differentiation explains why both perfectly competitive and monopolistic elements are to be found when observing modern markets:

> A general class of a product is differentiated if any significant basis exists for distinguishing the goods (or services) of one seller from those of another. Such a basis may be real or fancied, so long as it is of any importance whatever to buyers, and leads to a preference for one variety of the product over another. Where such differentiation exists, even though it be slight, buyers will be paired with sellers, not by chance and at random (as under pure competition), but according to their preferences.   (Chamberlin 1933: 56)

This kind of differentiation may be based on certain characteristics of the product itself – it could be the packaging, the available colours, the design or the style – but it could also be the conditions under which the sale takes place: the proximity of the seller's location, say, or the reputation of the seller. It is not difficult to find good contemporary examples: for instance, Apple products are differentiated from other brands by design and user friendliness (and, in consequence, also by their price). We also know that what is now called "marketing" and "branding" can be used to differentiate products from similar products provided by competitors. Where previously (in the works of authors such as Marshall) "monopolistic competition" denoted competition between a few very large firms (which is nowadays

---

$= P (1 + 1/\varepsilon)$ (where ε is a negative number). This relationship was already established by both Robinson (1933) and Amoroso (1930) and is therefore sometimes named "the Amoroso-Robinson relation". See Giocoli (2012) for more about the role of Amoroso.

known as "oligopolistic competition"), for Chamberlin it is a different form of industrial organization. For the monopoly firm, price (as determined by supplied quantities, given demand) was the relevant variable. In "monopolistic competition" two other variables are added: the nature of the product and advertising outlay (Chamberlin 1933: 71). The firm can still decide to change its price, but it can also provide a (slightly) differentiated product, and it can also use advertising to differentiate its product further.

Chamberlin's extensive analysis cannot be summarized in a few sentences, but it may be briefly characterized as follows. The perfectly competitive firm will simply take the market price as given, since all goods are homogeneous and consumers will buy from the cheapest seller. The monopolist will choose a price (which will determine, given the demand curve, its quantity to be sold) in such a way that profits are maximized (which is where marginal revenue equals marginal cost). The "monopolistically competitive" firm is somewhat in between: by raising its price it may lose some of its customers and by lowering its price the firm may attract more buyers, depending on the level of differentiation of the product. Like all firms, the monopolistically competitive firm will maximize profits by setting marginal revenue equal to marginal cost – it may, for instance, decide to lower its price in order to attract more buyers.

Chamberlin uses diagrams that include two demand curves: one for the case in which rivals keep their price constant, and one for the case in which rivals follow the price change. If a firm makes supernormal profits, other firms will be attracted to entering the market. The long-term equilibrium is then that firms charge a higher price (and sell a lower quantity) than in perfect competition, but they still charge a lower price (and correspondingly sell a higher quantity) compared with a monopoly.[13]

---

13. Chamberlin's approach has been heavily criticized, including by Friedman (1966: 38–9). The main argument is that there is a contradiction between, on the one hand, having firms with differentiated products, and on the other hand arguing that these firms are active in the same market, having identical cost and demand curves. "What does it mean to say that the cost and demand curves of a firm producing bulldozers are identical with those of a firm producing hairpins?" A different approach to differentiated goods was provided by Hotelling (1929), who represented different qualities of goods as if they were different locations (coming with different transportation costs for consumers), and used location analysis (based on Thünen's approach in his *Isolated State*) to determine equilibrium outcomes (where, again, all firms would maximize profits by setting marginal revenue equal to marginal cost). In this model firms would choose a certain differentiation of their product, corresponding to a certain location.

Imperfect competition and market structure

The field that studies imperfectly competitive market behaviour is now commonly called "industrial organization". Different market structures are identified based on the way in which firms compete with each other. A first approach is based on Cournot (1838) and assumes that firms are engaged in quantity competition. Every firm will set its quantity, by equating marginal revenue and marginal cost, on the assumption that the quantity set by rival firms remains constant. It can be shown that the Cournot equilibrium outcome leads to equilibrium prices that are higher than under perfect competition but lower than in monopoly. When more firms are added to the Cournot model, the equilibrium outcome will approach the perfectly competitive equilibrium.

Cournot's approach was criticized by the mathematician Joseph Bertrand, who published a critical review in 1883 about the use of mathematics within economic theory, by reviewing the works of both Cournot (1838) and Walras (1874). He argued that firms would compete in terms of price rather than quantity, and this approach has now become known as "Bertrand competition". Firms will try to grasp a bigger share of the market by undercutting the price of their rivals. Price competition in homogeneous goods will end up with the perfectly competitive outcome, since rival firms will continue to undercut each other until the price becomes equal to marginal cost.[14] This outcome occurs even if only two firms are active in the market. It is the same outcome as in perfect competition, while the perfectly competitive outcome is usually achieved by having a large number of active firms. This phenomenon is now commonly known as the "Bertrand paradox": price competition in homogeneous goods leads to the perfectly competitive equilibrium (i.e. market price is equal to marginal cost) even if only two firms are active in the market. In Bertrand or price competition, firms will again maximize their profits by equating marginal revenue and marginal cost, but now by assuming that rival firms keep their prices constant.

---

14. Note that, in a Bertrand price game, prices are determined simultaneously, i.e. all firms set their prices at the same time. For illustrative purposes, we have presented it here as a sequential process in which firms continue to undercut each other's price, until the level of marginal cost is reached. But in a simultaneous Bertrand price game, firms will foresee that this process would happen, and will therefore immediately set their prices at the level of marginal cost, as is also the case in perfect competition.

Yet another approach is derived from the German economist Heinrich von Stackelberg, whose *Market Structure and Equilibrium*, first published in German in 1934, takes into account that the market leader may set his quantity first, and this is then observed by the follower(s). This approach has been extended using game theory, which deals with strategic interaction between "players" of the "game": in this case firms that are trying to maximize their profits. Whereas in "Cournot quantity games" and "Bertrand price games" firms set their quantities or prices simultaneously (i.e. at the same time), in Stackelberg games the leader sets its quantities (or prices) first.

It is also possible to construct "mixed games", e.g. when firms determine their quantities in the first "round" and then "play a price game" in the second round. In every case the equalization of marginal revenues and marginal costs plays an important role, given that this is the fundamental rule for firms to maximize their profits. We can conclude that marginalism plays an important role in the subfield of "industrial organization", which grew out of the economics of imperfect competition.

Arthur Cecil Pigou and the economics of welfare

The early twentieth century is also the era during which "welfare economics" was established as another subfield in economic theory. Pigou, who studied under Marshall and later became his successor as professor of economics at the University of Cambridge, investigated the welfare implications of the modern economic system in his *The Economics of Welfare*, first published in 1920. According to Pigou, "economic welfare" is that part of welfare that can be measured in terms of money. "Welfare" is a much broader term and refers to "states of consciousness and, perhaps, their relations" (Pigou 1920: 10). These states of consciousness are concerned with satisfaction or dissatisfaction that members of society experience within (and because of) the economic system in which they participate. He focuses his attention on the "national income" or the "national dividend", which "include[s] everything that people buy with money income, together with the services that a man obtains from a house owned and inhabited by himself" (Pigou 1920: 34). Given that Pigou wants to investigate the economy at the societal level, he devotes a lot of space to clearly defining and measuring the national dividend.

Marginalism enters his analysis when he introduces the notion of "marginal social net product". Here, Pigou refers to Clark's analysis of marginalism (see chapter 7): "The marginal net product of a given quantity of resources is equal to the difference that would be made to the total product of these resources by adding to or subtracting from them a small increment" (Pigou 1920: 132). These resources and the national dividend are "flows" rather than "stocks", which means that they are recurring payments rather than piles of money.

In order to investigate these "flows", we must fix a certain period of time, such as a year. We can then investigate by how much the national dividend changes when a small increment is added to or subtracted from the quantity of resources. The flow of resources (both before and after the addition or subtraction of the small increment) must be "appropriately organized", which means that these resources must be used in the most efficient way. This implies that the increment of one of the factors of production (labour or capital) is not a particular unit (of labour or capital), nor is it the worst unit, as all units are exactly alike. So far, Pigou's analysis is very similar to Clark's theory. But the marginal product that we establish in this way is actually the "marginal *private* net product", or the increase in production caused by an increment in one of the resources that accrues to the person responsible for the investment. Since Pigou wants to investigate the economy and economic welfare at the level of society as a whole, he needs to introduce the "marginal *social* net product":

> The marginal social net product is the total net product of physical things or objective services due to the marginal increment of resources in any given use or place, no matter to whom any part of this product may accrue. (Pigou 1920: 134)

This implies that all effects caused by the increment need to be taken into account, even if they do not directly impact on the person doing the investment. These effects may be negative or positive "externalities", as they are called in contemporary microeconomic theory. For instance, a railway engine may generate sparks that damage surrounding woods. If this damage is uncompensated, then it will not impact the private product for the owner of the railway engine but it will negatively affect the social product. An example of positive externalities are economies of scale that are external to the firm, as discussed by Marshall. For instance, the existence of the railway may reduce the cost for businesses that are located near the railway stations. All these factors need to be taken into account in order to determine the "marginal social net product" of a certain resource: "In some conditions [the marginal private net product] is equal to, in some it is greater than, in others it is less than the marginal social net product" (Pigou 1920: 135).

At the societal level, an optimal allocation of resources implies that all "marginal social net products" must be equal everywhere, otherwise we could increase the national dividend by rearranging one or more of the resources (if we assume that there are no costs for moving these resources). This is clearly in line with what Jevons, Clark and other marginalists concluded earlier, except that the conception of "marginal social net product" also takes (negative and positive) externalities into account.

Even if a complete equality of all these "marginal social net products" cannot be achieved, a diminution in the degree of inequality between them will probably improve the national dividend.[15] If moving the resources is costly, then the gain in marginal social net product should exceed these movement costs.

Unfortunately, the desired social result is not always achieved by the "invisible hand". While self-interest tends to bring equality in the values of marginal *private* net products (since firms want to maximize their profits), this is not the case for marginal *social* net products (unless private and social are identical). If a business person wants to make a choice between different projects, including the railway mentioned above, then he or she will not take into account the damage caused by the sparks it generates. In this case, the marginal social net product will be smaller than the marginal

---

15. "Thus, if the distribution of resources is so altered that a number of values of marginal social net products which are below the average are all increased, or if a number which are above the average are all diminished, it is certain that the dividend will be increased. But, if a cause comes into play, which, while decreasing the degree of inequality among the values of marginal social net products on the whole, yet increases *some* values that are above the average and diminishes *some* that are below it, this is not certain. This type of difficulty is not, however, of great practical importance" (Pigou 1920: 137–8).

private net product because of negative externalities that are not paid for by the private investor. Another example would be the building of a factory in a residential area – in such a case, the marginal social net product may even be negative.

Marginal private net product may also fall short of marginal social net product in the case of positive externalities. There may be uncompensated benefits: when ships benefit from the light produced by a lighthouse but do not pay a toll, for instance, or when the government invests in a private park in order to improve air quality even if the general public is not allowed to enter the park. Another example is fundamental scientific research, which sometimes leads to unexpected benefits for industry and the economy in general.

The building of lighthouses, investment in private parks and fundamental scientific research would not occur if governments were unwilling to finance such activities, since the marginal private net product in these cases would be smaller than the marginal social net product. The government may decide to implement "extraordinary encouragements" (e.g. to stimulate fundamental scientific research) or "extraordinary restraints" (e.g. to prevent the building of factories in residential areas) through bounties or taxes.[16]

The government may decide to subsidize or even wholly fund fundamental scientific research but also services such as town planning, police administration or the clearing of slum areas – no private investor would find it profitable to do so. Building a factory in a residential area may be forbidden, or taxed so heavily that no investor would find the project profitable. In most countries, production and distribution of alcohol is taxed heavily, since it tends to generate a large private net product but a low social net product (given the negative externalities caused by drunkenness) (Pigou 1920: 183–96).[17]

Another important matter for welfare economics concerns the existence of monopolies. Given that the monopolist wants to maximize his profits, his output will be lower than it would be under perfect competition

---

16. In case the externalities occur between parties that are bound by contractual arrangements, then these contracts may be modified. This is not possible if the general public or society as a whole suffers or benefits from these externalities.
17. As Coase (1960) remarks, Pigou's analysis led to a new subfield of economic theory,

(Pigou 1920: 270). Given that the output will be lower, it must be the case that the price is higher. A lower output and a higher price imply that consumers will get less consumer surplus. As we saw in the previous chapter, consumer surplus is given by the sum of the differences (for all consumed units) between the willingness to pay of the consumer, and the market price that the consumer actually pays. Given that the willingness to pay is higher for "earlier" units, consumer surplus will be lower when fewer units are bought and when the market price is higher. All textbooks in microeconomics present the standard case of monopoly versus perfect competition. It can be shown, with geometry or algebra, that only part of the lost consumer surplus is transformed by the monopolist into surplus profits. The remaining part is lost, and is typically called the "deadweight loss" to society caused by the existence of the monopoly (compared with the case of perfect competition).

In terms of Pigou, we may also say that the monopolist increases his private net product (compared with the perfectly competitive outcome), but by less than the decrease of the social net product. The analysis of imperfect competition, which was discussed above, also has implications for economic welfare. For instance, the outcome of Chamberlin's model of imperfect competition is worse for consumers than the outcome under perfect competition (because the consumer surplus is lower), but it can be argued that it comes with more freedom to choose (since a greater variety of differentiated products is available to consumers).

---

welfare economics, in which it was generally thought that the project investor or the owner of the factory should be held liable for the damage caused, and that this situation should be solved by legislation and taxation. However, there is also the other side of the coin, which he illustrates with his well-known example of a doctor and a confectioner. The confectioner produces noise which prevents the doctor from having certain consultations with his patients. Following Pigou, the confectioner should be held liable, and he should either stop making the noise or pay the doctor a financial compensation. The point is, however, that in this case the confectioner would be harmed, as he would no longer be allowed to (fully) pursue his profitable activities. What really matters, is which activity contributes most to economic welfare. If the activity of the confectioner were to be more profitable than the activity of the doctor, then the confectioner could pay the doctor for not having his consultations, or for insulating his practice. If the doctor's consultations were more profitable, then he could pay the confectioner for terminating his business. This principle, which became known as the Coase theorem, indicates that the government is not required to settle disputes regarding externalities, provided that there are no significant bargaining costs. See for instance Frank (2013: 565–72 and 585–6) for a discussion with numerical examples.

Marginalism and macroeconomics: John Maynard Keynes

Another of Marshall's students was John Maynard Keynes, the founder of macroeconomics. While microeconomics deals with individual goods, markets, consumers and producers, macroeconomics looks at the economy from an "aggregate" point of view. Within macroeconomics we find concepts such as gross domestic product (GDP: the total value of goods and services produced within a country in a year), unemployment and inflation.

When Keynes wrote his *The General Theory of Employment, Interest and Money* (1936), his starting point was, by necessity, the economic theory available at that time: namely, microeconomics. It should therefore be no surprise to find marginalist concepts in his work. The main purpose of *The General Theory* was to find an explanation for the high levels of unemployment in the Western world during the 1930s, known as the Great Depression, which did not seem to disappear automatically through the working of the "invisible hand".

Keynes's starting point in *The General Theory* are the "postulates" (the most fundamental theoretical statements) of what he calls "classical economics" (with authors such as Ricardo, Mill, Marshall and Pigou lumped together).

- The first postulate is that "the wage is equal to the marginal product of labour". As we know from previous chapters (see, for example, the discussion of Clark's work), the wage rate should be equal to the marginal product of labour, which we can find by removing one unit of labour from the economic system and observing by how much total output decreases. Keynes agrees with this statement (provided that markets and competition are perfect).
- The second postulate is that "the utility of the wage when a given volume of Labour is employed is equal to the marginal disutility of that amount of employment" (Keynes 1936: 5). This second postulate can be explained by Jevons's theory of labour supply, which we discussed in chapter 4. Labourers will offer additional units of labour as long as the marginal utility of the wage exceeds the marginal disutility of the labour. But when the working day is lengthened (when the labourer supplies more labour), the marginal utility of the wage will diminish and the marginal disutility of labour will rise. Hence, in equilibrium,

the labourer will want to supply the amount of labour for which both are equal. Keynes does not agree with this argument, and therefore he rejects this second postulate. He disagrees because it cannot explain the situation of chronic unemployment that prevailed during the Great Depression, when he wrote *The General Theory*. For Keynes, the postulate is compatible with "frictional unemployment": the temporary situation of people who are between jobs. The postulate is also compatible with "voluntary unemployment": when labourers refuse to accept a payment that is in accordance with their labour productivity, or when legislation or collective bargaining prevent the labourer from accepting the payment. But since it is incompatible with "involuntary unemployment", Keynes does not accept this second postulate. Involuntary unemployment implies that labourers would like to supply labour at the existing wage rate but that they cannot find a job.[18]

Keynes's main argument to explain this situation is that entrepreneurs and workers negotiate about the nominal wage (or "money-wage") but not about the real wage, since they do not control the price level. Moreover, while labourers will usually resist a reduction in their nominal wages, they will not withdraw their labour when the prices of their wage goods increase (i.e. when inflation occurs, which implies a lower real wage given the nominal wage). Given that the nominal wage, and not the real wage, is determined by the bargains between employers and labourers, no equilibrium real wage is established that would eliminate all "involuntary unemployment". The reason for the enormous unemployment of the 1930s was not that people were not willing to work at the existing real wages, but that there were simply not enough jobs available because of insufficient "effective demand". In particular, private investment was too low. The government should have stepped in with government investment, in order to compensate for the lack of private investment.[19]

Two important "marginal" concepts can be found at the heart of Keynes's analysis. The consumption function – which refers not to the consumption

---

18. "Men are involuntarily unemployed if, in the event of a small rise in the price of wage-goods relatively to the money-wage, both the aggregate supply of labour willing to work for the current money-wage and the aggregate demand for it at that wage would be greater than the existing volume of employment" (Keynes 1936: 15).

19. "If the Treasury were to fill old bottles with banknotes, bury them at suitable depths in

of a specific individual but to the "aggregate" consumption of the economy as a whole – requires the concept of "marginal propensity to consume" (Keynes 1936: 115). This is the additional consumption within the economy if the national income grows by a small increment. Suppose that the national income grows (because of an increase in private investment or government spending) by an increment of €1 and that the marginal propensity to consume is 75 per cent. This implies that 75 cents of the additional €1 will be consumed and that the remaining 25 cents will be saved. The 75 cents that is spent will then become income for other people (i.e. the shopkeepers that sell goods and receive the 75 cents). The shopkeepers will then spend 75 per cent of the 75 cents, so 56.25 cents, which will again become income for somebody else. And so it continues. This implies that the additional €1 that is "injected" into the economy will increase national income by more than €1. The factor by which national income is increased is called the "investment multiplier", or simply the "multiplier": a fundamental concept in modern macroeconomics.[20]

Another concept used by Keynes is the "marginal efficiency of capital", which he defines as "being equal to that rate of discount which would make the present value of the series of annuities given by the returns expected from the capital-asset during its life just equal to its supply price" (Keynes 1936: 135). This can best be explained using a simple numerical example. Suppose that we have a project that, for every €1 that is invested now, will give us a return of €1.10 next year (i.e. we get our invested €1 back plus an additional 10 cents). The marginal efficiency of capital in this case would thus be 0.1, or 10 per cent. Keynes emphasizes that the concept is about

---

disused coal-mines which are then filled up to the surface with town rubbish, and leave it to private enterprise on well-tried principles of *laissez-faire* to dig the notes up again [...], there need be no more unemployment and, with the help of the repercussions, the real income of the community, and its capital wealth also, would probably become a good deal greater than it actually is. It would, indeed, be more sensible to build houses and the like; but if there are political and practical difficulties in the way of this, the above would be better than nothing" (Keynes 1936: 129).

20. Most textbooks in macroeconomics use a linear consumption function, given by $C = C_0 + c_1(Y_D)$, where C_0 is autonomous consumption (the consumption that would occur even if income were zero), c_1 is the marginal propensity to consume and Y_D is disposable income (income after taxes). It can be shown that the multiplier becomes $1/(1-c_1)$, which in our example of $c_1 = 0.75$ would give us a multiplier of 4. An increase in private investment or government spending of €1 would therefore increase national income by €4.

"expected" returns, and therefore has little to do with earlier notions of "perfect information".

Keynes uses marginalist concepts, but his most important departure from earlier authors is that he is sceptical about the ability of capitalist markets to automatically come to an equilibrium, especially in the labour market and in the market for money.[21] There is no perfect information and there is certainly no autopilot (or "invisible hand") that will automatically bring the economy into an equilibrium in which income (and welfare) are maximized.[22]

In chapter 18 of *The General Theory*, Keynes elaborates on the four "conditions of stability" that (in his view) explain why the economy did not automatically recover from the Great Depression (Keynes 1936: 245–54). Interestingly, his explanations are couched in marginalist terms.

1. The first condition states that the multiplier, while greater than one, cannot be very large. If the multiplier were very large, then just a small increase in private investment or government expenditure would "boost" the economy out of a crisis. As we have seen above, the multiplier is defined in terms of the marginal propensity to consume: a higher marginal propensity to consume implies a larger multiplier. When GDP increases (and people become richer), more of the additional income will be saved and the marginal propensity to consume will therefore go down, which will lower the multiplier. Experience shows that the economic system is not violently unstable and can remain in a "chronic condition of sub-normal activity for a considerable period", and therefore it must be the case that the multiplier is not very large (and hence, that the marginal propensity to consume is not too high).

2. The second condition states that a moderate change in expected future profits will not in great disproportion change the rate of investment.

---

21. For more about Keynes's criticism of marginalist theory, see for instance Kurz (2012).
22. Keynes also questions the rationality of (investment) decisions. "Even apart from the instability due to speculation, there is the instability due to the characteristic of human nature that a large proportion of our positive activities depend on spontaneous optimism rather than on a mathematical expectation […] Most, probably, of our decisions […] can only be taken as a result of animal spirits – of a spontaneous urge to action rather than inaction, and not as the outcome of a weighted average of quantitative benefits multiplied by quantitative probabilities" (Keynes 1936: 161).

As we saw above, the relationship between expected future profits and the rate of investment is given by the marginal efficiency of capital. An increase in expected future profits will indeed stimulate investment, but there will also be increasing costs, at least if the capital-assets are already fully utilized. Therefore, the marginal efficiency of capital expresses a positive relationship between expected future profits and rate of investment, but not to a disproportionate extent.

3. The third condition is merely about price stability: a change in (un)employment will not lead to a great change in wages (and prices). When GDP increases (more is being produced), employment will go up (and unemployment will go down), which will give workers a stronger bargaining position "because the bargaining position of the worker is improved and because the diminished marginal utility of his wage and his improved financial margin make him readier to run risks" (Keynes 1936: 253). Higher wages imply higher costs for firms, which implies that the firms will set higher prices. But if this reasoning were to apply, then we would see higher prices whenever unemployment fell. In order to explain that this does not occur, Keynes brings forward his "relative income hypothesis". He argues that workers will typically not care about the nominal wage per se, but rather about the "relative wage" (compared with colleagues and with workers in other industries). Furthermore, Keynes states that experience shows that the struggle for higher wages remains within limits (since we do not see a violent instability in the price level).

In summary, these three conditions express positive relationships between investment and GDP (the multiplier as determined by the marginal propensity to consume), between expected future profits and investment (the marginal efficiency of capital), and between GDP and prices (via unemployment and wages), but these positive relationships are rather small (as can be seen from experience), which explains the stability of the system.

4. The fourth condition is not about the stability of the system as such, but about the tendency of a fluctuation to reverse itself in due course. If investment remains low for an extended period of time, then fewer capital goods will be available and the marginal efficiency of capital will therefore go up. This will then, in turn, stimulate investment. On

the other hand, more investment will decrease the marginal efficiency of capital and will therefore discourage further investment.

We can conclude that Keynes's macroeconomic theory makes extensive use of marginalist conceptions. During the 1930s, marginalism evolved into a general framework of economic reasoning and formed the basis of a variety of subfields that are now distinct areas of research. The issues concerning the measurement of (marginal) utility were circumvented with the introduction of the "marginal rate of substitution", which led to the development of "indifference curves" and "indifference maps". The analysis of consumer choice was extended to intertemporal choice using the concept of "marginal rate of time preference", and it was extended to the analysis of optimal input choice for firms using the concept of "marginal rate of technical substitution". For the theory of the firm, the rule that "marginal revenue" must be equal to "marginal cost" in order to maximize profits became a general principle that would explain the behaviour of the firm. This rule applies to all market structures: not only perfect competition or monopoly, but also intermediate forms of "imperfect competition". Welfare economics extended the vocabulary with "marginal private net product" and "marginal social net product", which allows the study of welfare effects at the societal level. And although macroeconomic theory provided quite different insights about the market economy compared with earlier microeconomic approaches, at its core we find important concepts such as "marginal propensity to consume" and "marginal efficiency of capital". Marginalism became the backbone of economic theory.

Concluding remarks

This concludes our brief survey of the history of marginalism. I hope that this short exploration contributes to a more intuitive understanding of economic theory, which may complement the analytical understanding that is fostered by textbooks in (any subfield of) economics.

Thinking about the margin emerges on the supply side, where the scarcity of certain resources, particularly fertile land, implies diminishing marginal returns. Thinking about the margin also emerges on the demand side, where continued consumption implies diminishing marginal utility. These lines of thought examine the forces that underlie supply and demand, and lead up to a theory of exchange. This theory gave rise to a model of general equilibrium, which represents the interdependency between all markets, assuming that perfectly competitive conditions prevail. But marginalism is also relevant for the study of imperfect competition, which examines the consequences of substantial market power, usually exercised by a small number of large firms.

Marginalism can also be seen as a theory of economic decision-making, with a "process-oriented" and "subjective" approach. Marginalism is everywhere in modern economic theory, especially in microeconomics. But it is also relevant for macroeconomics, for welfare economics, for environmental economics – indeed, it would be hard, if not impossible, to imagine the field of economics without the central notions about the "margin".

Marginalism should probably not be seen as an economic "theory" as such, but rather as a "tool" that is visible in all fields and subfields of modern economics. And it should be seen as a "positive" tool, used to examine conditions of efficiency, and not as a "normative" tool, used to argue in favour of or against a certain distribution of income.

References

Amoroso, L. [1930] 1954. "The Static Supply Curve". In *International Economic Papers No. 4: Translations Prepared for the International Economic Association*, A. Peacock *et al.* (eds), pp. 39–65. Barcelona: International Economic Association.

Antognazza, M. 2016. *Leibniz: A Very Short Introduction*. Oxford: Oxford University Press.

Aquinas, T. 1948. *Summa Theologica*. New York: Benziger Bros.

Aristotle 1984. *Collected Works*. Princeton, NJ: Princeton University Press.

Arrow, K. & G. Debreu 1954. "Existence of an Equilibrium for a Competitive Economy". *Econometrica* 22(3): 265–90.

Backhouse, R. [2002] 2004. *The Ordinary Business of Life: A History of Economics from the Ancient World to the Twenty-First Century*. Princeton, NJ: Princeton University Press.

Bertrand, J. 1883. "Review of *Théorie mathématique de la richesse sociale* (Walras) & *Recherches sur les principes mathématiques de la théorie des richesses* (Cournot)". *Journal des Savants* 1883(September): 499–508.

Blaug, M. [1962] 1997. *Economic Theory in Retrospect*. Cambridge: Cambridge University Press.

Blaug, M. 1972. "Was There a Marginal Revolution?" *History of Political Economy* 4(2): 269–80.

Blaug, M. 1985. "The Economics of Johann von Thünen". *Research in the History of Economic Thought and Methodology* 3: 1–25.

Böhm-Bawerk, E. v. [1884] 1890. *Capital and Interest: A Critical History of Economic Theory*. London: Macmillan.

Boulding, K. 1971. "After Samuelson, Who Needs Adam Smith?" *History of Political Economy* 3(2): 225–37.

Bowman, R. 1989. "Jevons' Economic Theory in Relation to Social Change and Public Policy". *Journal of Economic Issues* 23(4): 1123–47.

Cartwright, E. [2011] 2018. *Behavioral Economics*. New York: Routledge.

Chamberlin, E. [1933] 1947. *The Theory of Monopolistic Competition: A Re-Orientation of the Theory of Value*. Cambridge, MA: Harvard University Press.

Clark, J. 1891. "Distribution as Determined by a Law of Rent". *Quarterly Journal of Economics* 5(3): 289–348.

Clark, J. [1899] 1908. *The Distribution of Wealth: A Theory of Wages, Interest and Profits*. London: Macmillan.

Coase, R. 1960. "The Problem of Social Cost". *Journal of Law & Economics* 3: 1–44.

Cohen, A. & G. Harcourt 2003. "Whatever Happened to the Cambridge Capital Theory Controversies?" *Journal of Economic Perspectives* 17(1): 199–214.

Cournot, A. [1838] 1897. *Researches into the Mathematical Principles of the Theory of Wealth*. London: Macmillan.

Crafts, N. & T. Mills 1994. "Trends in Real Wages in Britain, 1750–1913". *Explorations in Economic History* 31: 176–94.

Deane, P. 1989. *The State and the Economic System: An Introduction to the History of Political Economy*. Oxford: Oxford University Press.

Dobb, M. 1973. *Theories of Value and Distribution Since Adam Smith: Ideology and Economic Theory*. Cambridge: Cambridge University Press.

Driver, J. 2007. *Ethics: The Fundamentals*. Oxford: Blackwell.

Dupuit, J. [1844] 1952. "On the Measurement of the Utility of Public Works". *International Economic Papers* 2: 83–110. (Reprinted in 1969: *Readings in Welfare Economics*, K. Arrow & T. Scitovsky (eds). Homewood, IL: Richard D. Irwin.)

Edgeworth, F. 1881. *Mathematical Psychics: An Essay on the Application of Mathematics to the Social Sciences*. London: Kegan Paul.

Frank, R. & E. Cartwright 2013. *Microeconomics and Behaviour*. London: McGraw Hill.

Friedman, M. 1966. *Essays in Positive Economics*. Chicago, IL: University of Chicago Press.

Giocoli, N. 2012. "Who Invented the Lerner Index? Luigi Amoroso, the Dominant Firm Model, and the Measurement of Market Power". *Review of Industrial Organization* 41: 181–91.

Gossen, H. [1854] 1927. *Entwicklung der Gesetze des menschlichen Verkehrs und der daraus fliessenden Regeln für menschliches Handeln*. Berlin: Prager.

Heimann, E. [1945] 1964. *History of Economic Doctrines*. New York: Oxford University Press.

Hicks, J. 1934. "A Reconsideration of the Theory of Value. Part I". *Economica* 1(1): 52–76.

Hilferding, R. [1910] 1955. *Das Finanzkapital. Eine Studie über die jüngste Entwicklung des Kapitalismus*. Berlin: Dietz.

Hobson, J. 1891. "The Law of Three Rents". *Quarterly Journal of Economics* 5(3): 263–88.

Hotelling, H. 1929. "Stability in Competition". *Economic Journal* 39(153): 41–57.

Howey, R. 1972. "The Origins of Marginalism". *History of Political Economy* 4(2): 269–80.

Hutchison, T. 1978. *On Revolutions and Progress in Economic Knowledge*. Cambridge: Cambridge University Press.

Jaffé, W. 1976. "Menger, Jevons and Walras De-Homogenized". *Economic Inquiry* 14(4): 511–24.

Jensen, R. & N. Miller 2008. "Giffen Behaviour and Subsistence Consumption". *American Economic Review* 98(4): 1553–77.

Jevons, W. 1866. "Brief Account of a General Mathematical Theory of Political Economy". *Journal of the Royal Statistical Society London* 29: 282–87.

Jevons, W. [1871] 2001. *The Theory of Political Economy*, 1st edn. Writings on Economics, Volume 1. Basingstoke: Palgrave Macmillan.

Jevons, W. [1879] 2001. *The Theory of Political Economy*, 2nd edn. Writings on Economics, Volume 2. Basingstoke: Palgrave Macmillan.

Jolink, A. 1996. *The Evolutionist Economics of Léon Walras*. London: Routledge.

Jolink, A. & J. van Daal 1998. "Gossen's Laws". *History of Political Economy* 30(1): 43–50.

Keynes, J. [1936] 1951. *The General Theory of Employment, Interest and Money*. London: Macmillan.

Kurz, H. 2012. "Two Critics of Marginalist Theory: Piero Sraffa and John Maynard Keynes". *Investigacion Economica* 280: 23–54.

Landreth, H. & D. Colander 2002. *History of Economic Thought*. Boston, MA: Houghton Mifflin.

Leonard, T. 2003. "'A Certain Rude Honesty': John Bates Clark as a Pioneering Neoclassical Economist". *History of Political Economy* 35(3): 521–58.

Lerner, A. 1934. "The Concept of Monopoly and the Measurement of Monopoly Power". *Review of Economic Studies* 1(3): 157–75.

Longfield, M. 1834. *Lectures on Political Economy Delivered in Trinity and Michaelmas Terms, 1833*. Dublin: Richard Milliken & Son.

Malthus, T. [1798] 1985. *An Essay on the Principle of Population and a Summary View of the Principle of Population*. London: Penguin.

Marshall, A. [1890] 1997. *Principles of Economics*. Amherst, NY: Prometheus.

Marshall, A. [1919] 1932. *Industry and Trade: A Study of Industrial Technique and Business Organization; and of their Influence on the Conditions of Various Classes and Nations*. London: Macmillan.

Marx, K. [1867] 2010. *Capital*, Volume I. London: Lawrence & Wishart.

Meek, R. 1972. "Marginalism and Marxism". *History of Political Economy* 4(2): 499–511.

Menger, C. [1871] 1934. *Grundsätze der Volkswirtschaftslehre. The Collected Works of Carl Menger*, Volume I. London: London School of Economics & Political Science.

Mill, J. [1848] 1936. *Principles of Political Economy with Some of Their Applications to Social Philosophy*. London: Longmans, Green & Co.

Moscati, I. 2013. "Were Jevons, Menger, and Walras Really Cardinalists? On the Notion of Measurement in Utility Theory, Psychology, Mathematics, and Other Disciplines, 1870–1910". *History of Political Economy* 45(3): 373–414.

Mosselmans, B. 2007. *William Stanley Jevons and the Cutting Edge of Economics*. London: Routledge.

Nichol, A. 1934. "Robinson's Economics of Imperfect Competition". *Journal of Political Economy* 42(2): 257–59.

Pareto, V. [1906] 1919. *Manuale de economia politica con una introduzione alla scienza sociale*. Milano: Societa Editrice Libraria.

Paul, E. 1979. *Moral Revolution and Economic Science: The Demise of Laissez-Faire in Nineteenth-Century British Political Economy*. Westport, CT: Greenwood.

Petty, W. [1672] 1899. "The Political Anatomy of Ireland". In *The Economic Writings of Sir William Petty*, Volume 1. Cambridge: Cambridge University Press.

Petty, W. [1676] 1899. "Political Arithmetic". In *The Economic Writings of Sir William Petty*, Volume 1. Cambridge: Cambridge University Press.

Pigou, A. [1920] 1932. *The Economics of Welfare*. London: Macmillan.

Pullen, J. [2010] 2014. *The Marginal Productivity Theory of Distribution: A Critical History*. London: Routledge.

Raffaelli, T. 2002. *Marshall's Evolutionary Economics*. London: Routledge.

Ricardo, D. [1817] 1911/1996. *Principles of Political Economy and Taxation*. Amherst, NY: Prometheus.

Robinson, J. [1933] 1946. *The Economics of Imperfect Competition*. London: Macmillan.

Schumpeter, J. [1954] 1997. *History of Economic Analysis*. London: Allen & Unwin.

Shields, C. 2016. "Aristotle". In *Stanford Encyclopedia of Philosophy*, Edward N. Zalta (ed.), Winter 2016 edn. Available at https://plato.stanford.edu/archives/win2016/entries/aristotle/ (accessed 31 May 2018).

Smith, A. [1776] 1994. *An Inquiry into the Nature and Causes of the Wealth of Nations*. New York: Modern Library.

Soudek, J. 1952. "Aristotle's Theory of Exchange". *Proceedings of the American Philosophical Society* 96: 45–75.

Stackelberg, H. v. 1934. *Marktform und Gleichgewicht*. Wien: Springer.

Stigler, G. 1958. "Ricardo and the 93% Labour Theory of Value". *American Economic Review* 48(3): 357–67.

Stigler, G. & D. Becker 1977. "De Gustibus Non Est Disputandum". *American Economic Review* 67(2): 76–90.

Streissler, E. 1972. "To What Extent Was the Austrian School Marginalist?" *History of Political Economy* 4(2): 426–41.

Streissler, E. 1990. "The Influence of German Economics on the Work of Menger and Marshall". In *Carl Menger and His Legacy in Economics*, B. Caldwell (ed.). *History of Political Economy*, Annual Supplement to Volume 22: 31–68. Durham, NC: Duke University Press.

Thünen, J. v. [1850] 1910. *Der isolierte Staat in Beziehung auf Landwirtschaft und Nationalökonomie. Zweiter Teil. Der naturgemässe Arbeitslohn und dessen Verhältnis zum Zinsfuss und zur Landrente*. Jena: Verlag von Gustav Fischer.

Vorzimmer, P. 1969. "Darwin, Malthus and the Theory of Natural Selection". *Journal of the History of Ideas* 30(4): 527–42.

Walker, F. 1891. "The Doctrine of Rent, and the Residual Claimant Theory of Wages". *Quarterly Journal of Economics* 5(4): 417–37.

Walras, L. [1874] 1926/1969. *Elements of Pure Economics, or the Theory of Social Wealth*. New York: Kelley.

Walras, L. [1874] 1988. *Eléments d'économie politique pure ou théorie de la richesse sociale. Oeuvres Economiques Complètes*, Volume VIII. Paris: Economica.

White, M. 1989. "Why Are There No Supply and Demand Curves in Jevons?" *History of Political Economy* 21(3): 425–56.

White, M. 1991. "Jevons' 'Blunder' Concerning Value and Distribution: An Explanation". *Cambridge Journal of Economics* 15: 149–60.

Wieser, F. v. [1889] 1893. *Natural Value*. London: Macmillan.

Winch, D. 1972. "Marginalism and the Boundaries of Economic Science". *History of Political Economy* 4(2): 325–43.

Index